MW00884716

TO ASHLIE

w/ love

6/4/19

THANK YOU FOR BLESSING
MY LIFE W/ ANOTHER
ASHLIE! WE'RE NAME
TWINS & FRIENDS!
YOU ARE LOVED BY ME!

1

"While masterfully manipulating every tool, poetry gave me permission to break all the rules!"

-Ashley Nicole

Other People's Problems

Copyright © 2018

Sharing Is Karen Publishing and Life Coaching

Ordering Information:

Quantity sales. Special discounts are available on quantity purchases by corporations, associations, and others. For details, contact the publisher at the email address below.

Orders by U.S. trade bookstores and wholesalers. Please contact

SharingisKarenPublishingandLC@gmail.com

Printed in the United States of America

Title of book: Other People's Problems / Ashley Nicole

ISBN: 978-1544265520

First Edition

Rest in Paradise Uncle Ronnie

September 4, 1948- August 13, 2016

Never Thought That I Would Have To Miss You

I never knew that forever meant that I would never hear hello from you
again.

My eyes well up knowing you will never show up,

and cease to grow up with me as my friend.

My family you silently tore apart when you went from me.

My tattered heart slowly breaks as you take away my peace from me;

while you sleep peacefully.

My mind can't wrap around the thought of moving on from you,

my love belongs to you.

Short lived are the dreams that were planned for tomorrow.

Now my yesterday's I cherish in sorrow,

Other People's Problems

in hopes that relief will follow my pain.

Your name now etched in completion,

I find discomfort in my attempted deletion of your voicemails.

How unfair that the life we shared now humbly removed.

I disapprove the thought of never feeling another embrace.

My limbs tremble as I struggle to remember your face.

And it's just hard to embrace that you will never come back to me.

I know it's not that you've turned your back on me,

but as you lay silently I feel hopelessly abandoned.

How could God's will for your life feel so random and miscalculated.

They claim that now your life should be celebrated but I'm devastated,

and lack the ability to comprehend,

that now all of my yesterday's spent with my friend have now ended.

I will always love and try not to forget you,

and although my selfish thoughts will try to neglect you,

I'm just trying to find balance between respecting your memories,

and forgetting my miseries.

Your absence brings misery and now I have to love you differently.

I love who you were to me,

and although I wish you still were with me,

your memory will live on fervently;

Just forgive me for not understanding currently.

Preface:

When I decided to delve into the journey of creating this piece, I started with hopes of helping others with their personal problems by becoming completely transparent about mine. I have come to find that help comes in the form of relation and providing understanding; so the best that I can hope for when it comes to anyone who chooses to pick this book up, is that you feel a connection between our issues that assures you that you are not alone in your struggle, and that the gesture of publishing most of my painful moments in life is a part of my healing process; know that the deeper I go into understanding myself that I will be ultimately and intentionally attempting to help you do the same. The farther we walk away from our problems only leaves our deepest fears and insecurities to wonder where those lost moments of hope may be lingering. We must practice the art of asking ourselves why, when our intuition says no. Not for the sake of becoming belligerent to our own mental health, but in order to track down the seeds of disappointments in our past so that we may expel them of their trumped up power. We are unpredictable vessels that require love, nourishment, and maintenance daily. I urge you to excitedly pursue what maintains you, and to turn the volume down on life when it starts to drown out the existence of your voice and your truth. Practice the art of constantly loving yourself, and know that when you're loving you, you are also loving God.

Table of Contents

Other People's Problems

Other People's Problems

No Longer

I no longer require your warm shoulders on cold evenings,

spent dreaming of your potential.

This mental process of emancipation

no longer falls for infatuation,

accompanied by cute faces and heart races where I have lost every round.

The sound of stop by's equate faint cries in the distance,

where I foresee the lies of longevity in this union.

I feel better alone for now.

Not lonely,

at least not anymore after a wise man told me that I was completed when I was created.

Feel free to delete ex boyfriends you hated,

and evolve intrinsically through subtle interactions.

Where polite conversation doesn't invoke the impaction of matrimonious murmurs and meditations.

Where relations involve the meeting of the minds,

rather than his pelvis to your behind,

because that kind of love is mindfully temporary.

Scary are the thoughts of a single woman.

Sad are the multiple avenues toward our projected failures,

if it doesn't include the likes of Luke or Taylor in our everlasting ever after.

Yet, never have I ever felt love for me after love.

Never have I tasted the passion fruit of leftovers for fear of being left over there without my him.

I believe I'm ready to feel differently.

Other People's Problems

Rather than loving another sinfully,

I will excitedly love myself,

because, you see, it's not your help that I need anymore.

I can make my own trips to the store for tampons, licorice, and redbox movies.

Provide my own Christmas gifts, flowers, and jewelry.

No longer do I worry about broke men who ignore restaurant checks.

I'll avoid silly arguments over food because you don't know what you want yet.

I have no time for fortune tellers with big dreams and no focus.

No you cannot ride around in my car;

exchanging car keys for bus tokens.

I don't wanna chill at your house in the evening turning temptation into sex scenes.

So irritated by these overrated boys who constantly need a pic from me.

So sorry to the studs,

I won't be coming out to play,

and to the ones I've never been attracted to,

I will never see you that way.

and to you constant inconsistents with multiple women at a time,

go tend to your flock,

leave me alone,

and please stay off of my line.

My time is so precious,

and for now I'd rather be alone.

And your misguided intentions I will no longer condone.

Other People's Problems

I will date myself and place myself

at the top of my own priorities.

Who cares that you think I may be bitter

for giving you no room to love me more than me.

And to you happily devoted couples,

I am more than happy for you.

I just pray the discernment of your heart

lets you know whether or not

if bae was created just for you.

I don't want to keep any man who doesn't want to be kept,

and I hate the idea of imprisoned relationships where my heart has already
left.

And although I'm having a love affair with food

and I'm 20 pounds overweight,

I will embrace my gut

and my big butt

and love me now before it's too late.

I've chopped off my hair

so there will be no more perm,

Now all of my ideals of beauty will now have to be relearned.

To my so-called friends I am too loud

and my conversations never seem to end,

but that's ok I've solved that problem;

I found some better friends.

I also have a little pug

whose as cute as a bug,

Other People's Problems

And whenever I come home she shows me so much love.

And to the loved ones in my life

who sometimes fail to make appearances,

Sometimes I fail too,

but I'll always love you,

I will reach out when I think of you, period.

And as for my family that I'm getting to know,

You are the reason I know what love is

I just pray my reciprocation has shown.

Now I know it may seem that I have gone off track,

but the essence of feeling lonely takes place in every area that you may lack,

Love,

In your own life.

You are a powerful pristine production

that goes beyond just becoming some man's wife.

Loneliness is the devil's ploy to divide you from functional relationships.

Acknowledge other connections in your life,

don't settle for monsters for the sake of companionship.

Be convinced of your confidence and remember to smile.

Don't sweat the fact that you haven't dated in a while.

Remember what you want before making any decision.

Don't settle for almost's, could-be's, and blurry visions.

Be clear and concise.

You don't have to be nice.

Feel at peace while in your single hood,

15

Other People's Problems

don't use bitterness as a vice.

Embrace terms like I haven't shaved in awhile.

Feel free to smile back when you witness a smile.

Right now sex should not be associated with ample.

You are a treasured piece of merchandise,

you are not a free sample.

You were all physically created by a king in perfection,

so dismiss all who don't prefer you,

they're not qualified to sit in your section.

Money can't buy love and it should not buy your soul,

So reevaluate your motives while setting relationship goals.

Don't be fooled by the nice ones either,

it is al   so another trick.

Being nice is a good quality,

but that doesn't mean he's a good fit.

When you fall for love make sure you shoot for their spirit.

sexual love doesn't last and I know you don't wanna hear it.

Find a man with courageous convictions,

who shares your beliefs,

and never would,

find fault in putting God first.

He will do his best to treat you right,

simply because God said he should.

I know on the outside we can all be cool and confident,

but inside we wear singleness in shame.

Other People's Problems

So I suggest you apprehend this opportunity

to opt for peace and joy instead of hurt and pain.

Good bye relational incarceration!

Hello harmless flirtation!

Validate yourself through self-actualization!

Good times are on the brink of your imagination!

Release yourself from heart and mind manipulations!

And don't consider self alone you're just on a man vacation!

Words-4-tha-Wise- Embracing Singleness:

1. Find something to focus on and incorporate balance

2. Utilize this time to be active and interactive with others

3. Set high goals and accomplish them

4. Take time to foster your creative thoughts

5. Realize that your schedule belongs to you -- Have fun!

6. SAVE YOUR MONEY/Become established

7. Do what you would like to do in life without compromise

8. Spend more time with your family

9. Spend more time with your friends

10. Explore your city or even the world

Pardon My Pounds

Standing heavy and unrested,

I stand big breasted with ample posterities.

I too share thoughts of chocolates,

caramels and colorful taffies,

fast food restaurants, chips, and cookies

with those of you,

who too

share issues watching their weight.

Leaving my insecurities dormant,

and my will to change insubordinate,

I tend to act as though I love myself

every time I shove myself

into a gym,

into old clothes,

into the company of who I used to know.

But what I do know

is that my weight won't wait for me to change.

So I feel strange every time I climb atop a scale

in hopes of dissipating calories.

Praying that parking lot spots in the back,

or the waist trimmer wrapped around my back,

has worked its magic on me.

Praying that ultimately and immediately I might be smaller like I was.

More in shape like I used to be.

Other People's Problems

Thinner than I am now.

I conjure calculations in my head,

on how to lose the weight of my arms and legs,

simply by breathing air and drinking water.

Every once in awhile,

on my jog,

may I trudge a little farther.

Until I reach my sweet spot,

where sugary sweets wear the devil's cologne.

Where I will not shamefully condone that ritual of gluttony.

Where I do not stuff in me,

what's in front of me,

and for moments feel as if I deserved to feel full.

What is full anyway?

Proportions meant for distortions,

or smaller pieces of my original plated picture.

Apparently my salad plates are filled with too much ranch dressing,

to the point where I begin new workout plans when I start undressing every night.

Because I must maintain the sexy throughout all ages.

I must attain the discipline that will wipe away all pages

of saturated fats,

sugars, and serving sizes.

I want to be the image of emulation and appropriation

when it comes to my agility and ability to construct the bod-ess of a Goddess.

Other People's Problems

Who wouldn't want to sit peaked on a pedestal of adornment and
superiority?

While admiring adoringly

the fact that it shows that I am in love with myself.

I'd love myself so much that I'd be willing to do anything for it,

with it,

to it,

in order to make it congruent with better.

Because now I know better.

Comfy couches and warm beddings block my heart

from letting my soul be loosed of this weight that I carry.

For every pound I outweigh, that is another scar of decay on my spirit,

for I want to be near it.

Hating lunches where dates consume insurmountable amounts,

while I just take a salad.

I'm hungry too!

I'm tired of feeding myself lies,

tired of eating French fries,

tired of quitting on all my tries

to be a better and fitter version of me.

Ashamed of valuing myself by numbers on scales

while pounds sit on mounds outside my front door.

So I will step outside of myself in order to take care of myself,

in order to make sure my health and love for self is restored.

Words-4-tha-Wise- Overcoming Self Body Shaming:

1. Heal your body through proper nutrition

2. Ask yourself if you are hungry or just bored

3. Refrain from body shaming others

4. Understand that you are unique and beautiful anyway

5. Find comfort in yourself

6. Spend time with people who love you the way you are

7. Fall in love with yourself

8. Be patient

9. Always take the stairs

10. Take care of yourself

Miss-Carried Away

Life is reborn and re-given everyday,

but she is deprived of the life of her own giving;

and that sometimes makes life seem not worth living.

Just shifting the measure of life,

the span of time of which one can call herself a mother,

but no.

Just like every other infant-less person,

I now share their burdens,

their sorrows,

and wish that I may borrow an egg that won't break.

A soul he won't take away from me.

Tearing a piece of me apart.

Gently stabbing at my heart.

But again and again and again I heal

but still feel

the pain of yesterday's tomorrows.

I, why?

Now cry tears.

Tears of a broken spirit,

but you will never hear it.

Because I now fear the product of waking up and facing every single tomorrow.

No perscriptions strong enough to uplift my sorrows.

And now I lay,

the mother of a motherless child and pray,

that I don't grow the strength to venture this task again,

and lose another win.

Lord please, Forgive me.

Words-4-tha-Wise- Overcoming A Miscarriage:

1. Allow yourself to feel what you feel

2. Take your time if you are not ready to talk about it

3. An early miscarriage is common

4. A late miscarriage will most likely be harder to come to terms with

5. Many miscarriages happen for no reason at all

6. Take time off from your life to rest

7. Give your partner time to mourn

8. Surround yourself with loved ones

9. Find the courage to share your story with someone else

10. Seek professional advice if you choose to try again

A Dream

A dream is like a drug because it takes you away.

It is the cure to your late night hunger pains.

It heats up the blood pumping through your veins,

and drowns your very being in acid rain.

Suggests not to walk away from the speeding train,

and promotes self denial in order to deal with life's pain.

Makes you curious of the heat that seers over an open flame.

Makes your adrenaline high like a flying plane.

Keeps you wild to the point where you can't be tamed.

Forces you to laugh when you cry over growing pains.

To be in a zone with no thought of change.

To finally awake and find that life is still the same.

Words-4-tha-Wise- Walking Away From Intoxicants:

1. Allow yourself to bare your emotional pain

2. Spend time with friends and family

3. Share your fears about relapsing

4. Try healthy activities that are completely consuming

5. Practice the art of saying no

6. Stop before you start

7. Stay away from those who still do drugs

8. Reflect on why you may be tempted

9. Understand that you may have to quit by yourself

10. Find support

For, Not 1, But 2

You never learn hate for self until you make yourself do the unjust.

Unthoughtful crimes against existence.

My nerves take away resistence as I walk down sterilized halls of depression.

Yet I am oddly optimistic of what lies ahead.

"At least I'll have my life!" I'd say.

"At least it's just this one life I pray!"

Why now?

I ask,

but I know my past.

My lack of sense.

My knack for suspense.

My need to be loved,

understood,

adored and more.

Why now?

As I walk through creaking doors.

Pass over soundless floors.

Now and forever I'll hate that day.

No longer will I long for the month of my birthday.

Oh not 1 you say -- but 2!

1 pair of lives.

2 careless teens who demean the very value of intelligent thought.

Oh but that person we surely bought.

Ultrasound pictures stain my mind.

Other People's Problems

Make my ways seem unkind.

make my words slim to none,

for I have no tongue.

I didn't speak up for the two who could've been.

Their lives were never started,

but now with them I am departed.

Killing a piece of me daily.

Thinking that maybe,

I could have cared a little more.

Not thinking of what lied in store,

for, not 1, but 3,

placing 2 before me.

Wishing that one-day their might be a sparkle inside of me

to take place of the ones that got away.

The ones who couldn't stay.

Yet still everyday I think of what might have been.

The loves of my life,

my carrying kin.

That would glorify my features,

wear name brand sneakers,

And live as life's teachers.

Instead I cry at night,

writing pain through my lamp light.

Yesterday's glow,

will never know

Other People's Problems

how to love in that way.

But will always remember that day.

Always hate that urge to splurge hidden aspects of sexuality.

Use a little morality.

Then I wouldn't have to be sitting in that same chair,

losing locks of my hair.

I'll always remember those few shared moments,

me alone with my little components.

Opponents in which I'd sing to,

minutes I would seem to cling to,

never alone yet never felt you,

never held you.

No one could ever understand,

the love/hate I had for that man.

You never really feel by yourself until you allow yourself to feel things no one else has ever felt.

Although felt before, by many more.

No one,

for sure,

could ever endure the pain you gave to yourself that day.

Occasional thoughts but permanent love,

shall grasp my hearts in the grave I dug

for 1 and 2,

this one is for both of you.

Would trade it all so that you knew,

to never forget that mommy loves you.

30

<u>Words-4-tha-Wise- Abortion Aftermath:</u>

1. Acknowledge that this option is your choice

2. Feeling regret is normal

3. Share this difficult time with a loved one you trust

4. Don´t let what you believe beat you up about your decision

5. Revisit why you may have wanted an abortion in the first place

6. Itś ok to realize that you may not be ready to be a parent

7. Fearing pregnancy and childbirth is common

8. This kind of decision is a heavy one to make

9. Identify your first step towards moving forward

10. Seek professional advice if your are not well physically/mentally

Fall Back

Can't seem to understand why life feels this way.

Words seem to stay in my mouth,

in my mind,

where often I seem to find

that I'm not ok right now,

but I'm not at my worst right now.

But how do I keep finding reasons to be upset?

Hold on to things I cannot forget.

But yet I can't seem to shake this state.

I'm not stressed but there's a weight

on my shoulders that I need to release.

Find some restraint and gain some peace.

Find strength within my soul,

for I feel the need to dwell on what makes me unwell.

Distraught thoughts pollute my path,

my journey to righteousness.

Yet my foolishness won't let me walk towards the light,

live my life right,

stop crying at night,

so that one day I may take flights to different skies.

New lands,

new places,

find comfort in different and unfamiliar faces.

Because the familiar ones of which I am used to,

Other People's Problems

refuse to,

let me live comfortably.

At least let me find eternal peace.

And now my levels start to decrease.

Things once held high are now low.

Things I don't care to share seem to show.

My river of contemplation doesn't seem to flow anymore.

No time to wonder what purpose is stored within significants in my life

that aren't so significant.

FInding ridiculous excuses for why I need to get over,

get sober,

re-frame from hangovers,

that hangover my head for the past two years.

I've shed more than two tears.

My fear is not that I am fearful, but that I am inadequate.

Can't level out my deficits that lie deep within my pours.

I seem to pick up signals yet not through phones,

while monsters try to talk to me in vulgar tones.

As if that is my only function.

My only reason for being woman.

Bearing breast and hips,

with tender lips that do what?

I always seem to amuse the likes of those who are not worthy,

people that do not concern me.

People that do not show concern for me.

Other People's Problems

Why is this a life I live?

While others lie and give

me headaches for trying to be a part.

That makes me want to start going off on different tangents;

lines that connect to the circle but don't have a specific direction,

or a designated reason to move forward or not at all.

Because after all you only move if you feel it's necessary.

One only talks because silence is scary.

Only competing because outcomes may vary,

but I love so very very hard.

I don't feel as if I should discard my feelings,

but to pass out my everything is what I do.

With thoughts of you,

because it's all for you.

The me can wait as long as your needs are praised.

I'll be good I'll keep still because in the end I will always feel like I'm not giving enough,

as I keep on giving it up to you.

Or anyone for that matter,

then again none of this matters.

I'm about me, my work, and education

of which I dedicate my dedication.

But like inflation I will rise as time goes on goes by

because I am a woman of higher standards,

but momentarily I forgot what that meant.

I lent myself to others to hold me,

Other People's Problems

to make me feel like I once did before,

and two times before that.

I no longer seem to keep track,

so on my guard and support, I fall back.

Words-4-tha-Wise- Overcoming Uncertainty In Your Life:

1. Fear inhibits good decision making

2. Diagnose your fears to see if they are rational

3. Make a list of all of the things you know and don´t know

4. Embrace that there are things in life that are outside of our control

5. Know what matters and what does not

6. Do not seek perfection

7. Always have a contingency plan

8. Never ask "What if?"

9. Remain calm and breathe

10. Stay positive

Three Strings

Three strings once played the chords of my soul;

and all of what was in our control,

was the mold of my movement.

I was happy.

I was showered with love from the two that knew there was an "us" before any other "who" could come forth.

They loved me.

They loved each other.

He loved my mother like a King would love his Queen;

loved me like no man or anything could ever come before us.

It was his trust that brought us security.

It was his thrust of brute masculinity.

It was his lust that broke our family.

My heart stopped and I loved no more;

I had my own sense of reality.

I trolliped unhappily all the while knowing my sanity was based on a lie.

The triangle I knew to be us was doomed to bust at the thought of her.

Her is She.

She is the reason why we are no longer a family.

I wipe my tears.

I used to grab him cold beers from the refrigerator when I was a child.

That was then.

Even back then,

when I cheered,

and he encouraged me to overcome fears of public performance.

Other People's Problems

I would frolic in adornment of my father.

"You are the smartest A in the apple tree, the brightest B in the hive,

and C when used correctly you're the cutest thing alive"

he would say to me.

He saved me from low self-esteem.

Yet I can't help but remember his love being a bit harsh.

He banned me from visions of his own young testosterone driven
reflections staring at the grasses of my highschool yard.

To the members of my opposite sex he was my bodyguard;

to guard me from everything that could taint or paint pictures of horrid
images that would leave me uncared for,

unloved or,

possibly left in ruin.

Yet he is the man who ruined my life.

What about my mother?

As much as I would love to stab him with images of not caring he probably
cared too much;

Fearing that the honesty of his betrayal would be too much;

Fearing my mother would get fed up,

and leave.

He never wanted to give up or let go of our harmony.

For that I'm sorry.

Sorry you had to live up to being the man in all of our lives;

sorry we exiled you for all of your lies;

while you made tangent lines for a secretive fourth addition;

them.

Other People's Problems

His thoughtless acts plagued our mission toward happiness with sorrow.

He drowned our hopes for tomorrow.

He let her steal the love that she borrowed from my father.

She was selfish.

She didn't see it fit to leave our trinity be;

she had to play a part in our hearts

as if seemingly caring about the part

where she took my dad.

Ruining the union he had with my mother;

their flames sadistically smothered.

No love cold enough,

no lies old enough,

no life as hard or rough as the one I've been having these past couple of years.

You played roles of deception praying the eyes of peering innocents would never lead on to the conception of such thoughts of neglection;

neglecting morals,

standards where you choose to stand for something outside yourself;

where you learn to care for others outside yourself;

where you yearn to feel the love that was meant for yourself.

But you stand for nothing and therefore mean all of nothing to me.

And in my life you can't be;

in my future, you, I cannot see.

Forgiveness for you I hold deep within my mind,

somehow never stomaching the strength or emotion to want to find or give it to you.

Other People's Problems

My love for my family ran deep,

and deep within my head while I'm sleep I can only remember what we used to be,

instead of visualizing what we are.

For when I'm awake it is the memories that make me sad;

break me down;

take me back to days of ponytails and elbow scrapes that were kissed away with "all-betters",

and it hurts even worse because it's not all better, is it??

Instead it's better left alone.

For it is us you left alone.

The ones who cussed and fussed at your displays with disapproval,

being coward to conflict you inflicted the removal

of our song by removing one chord.

As if taking a sword to our wrists as we held hands.

Making plans of long thought of vacations,

reminiscing on old duty stations,

and playing songs that reignite the thought of celebration

that occurred when it came to the union of what we were.

I will always hate you for that.

I will always hate the fact that I hate you.

While further leaning away from our breakthroughs to your destination;

I have declared you the nonliving.

After all you are no longer living among us.

you moved toward a life that's new,

and it's really hard to wish I really knew what you were running from;

Other People's Problems

so instead I will run from you.

I stumble in thought.

Fickle in my walk from you

I'm ambushed by chocolate vanilla swirl afternoons.

My heart forces me to remember the wonderful father that never told me no,

while my mind remembers the man who chastised my feelings.

Who never took seriously the meaning of soft speaking

for my drums are bleeding from your baritone.

Never toning down,

you have sensitized my frowns.

Now at the mere whimper of a cat

I grit my teeth and think back

on days when I held my head to my knees,

while my tears formed oceans at my feet.

Mother always managing to omit your faults,

so that the stares from others would never smother the fire of our strength,

for they don't know the function of our home;

even if it is dysfunctional.

I laugh and cry at the same time.

Although your presence is no longer near and you manage to ignore every veer or grasp in your direction,

it is your lack of affection that resulted in the revival of my mother.

For it was your love that hurt and smothered her ability to rise;

that stutter stepped her walk with god,

and although it is still your job to stay until forever.

Other People's Problems

I would never want to relive your sabotage,

or your camouflaged case of skeletons that aren't your fault.

My heart will love my daddy forever,

but it is your absence that makes us better.

Although I once thought you'd leave us never,

nothing but pain existed while we were together.

Our distaste and distrust for your character are sure and certain.

We have closed the curtains on that three that made life make sense in my world.

now a little off balance and without,

we have found our way out from beneath your tyranny.

But I love you unconditionally

and my heart grows exponentially.

Praying you'll someday learn what unity means,

and for now our union lays ripped at the seams

I now know true life doesn't follow all dreams,

but you may remain in mines.

Words-4-tha-Wise- Finding Forgiveness:

1. Know that forgiveness is a choice

2. Acknowledge that you feel pain because you were hurt

3. Make a list of the things that have hurt you and explain why they were not ok

4. Commit to doing things that make you feel better

5. Your issues are not with the action, but your thoughts about the actions that took place

6. You are in control of your own thoughts

7. Practice stress reduction techniques when you feel yourself becoming upset

8. Practice gratitude daily

9. Know that the best revenge is a life well lived

10. Build a closer relationship with God

Missing My Daddy

Thank you for calling,

Goodbye.

no relief or concern for my cries.

Empty phone calls and convos denied for the sake of himself.

His pride won't let me,

and breaks me from him.

No entirety or fullness behind my grin,

my sin speaks out in lashes.

No missed calls before, during, or after classes.

He thrashes the time that I seek,

leaves us guessing,

confronting his streaks of absences,

that never used to occur.

Yet now without us is what he prefers.

His life has long run and fell short,

two broken homes with children left at port,

on their own devices,

but my boat is the last neglected.

Empty visions of my father reflected,

I just want my love to overcome his selfishness,

so that he sees the cold side of loneliness,

and realizes there is no sense in his nonsense,

and returns to the home of his preference.

Forsaken by many but loved unconditionally by one.

Other People's Problems

No amount of disappointment could make me run,

one son to call on, other daughters hide your mess,

and to me your half my world in one sense.

In another your all of my pride.

my whole life I've watched you protect and provide,

so for you my love I cannot hide,

and all problems, for you, I put aside.

I just want you to know with me there is a home

for those days when you feel all alone,

as if the world is a burden you must roam.

By your side is my designated zone.

Now I can say I don't appreciate the lies,

lonely nites and the times you've made us cry,

but for you I swallow tears and clinch my sighs,

just so you know you no longer have to hide.

You're the man that I've loved all my life,

killing spiders and rubbing tummies at night,

clothing, feeding, and ironing my tidy whites,

my heart stays true to get through to you every night

because you are my life.

Words-4-tha-Wise- Dealing With Daddy Issues:

1. Acknowledge that there is an emotional wedge between you and your father

2. Understand that any human can fall short and disappoint you

3. Be patient with yourself

4. Be completely honest with yourself and your father

5. Let go of people pleasing in order to fill a void

6. Reach out to your parent in a positive way often

7. Your Daddy may have "Daddy issues" of his own

8. Seek counseling from a neutral point of view

9. Continue to live your best life

10. Forgive

Unsure

All of this working on myself is changing me into something I am not.

I can understand that I'm maturing,

but why live with a self who is pleasing to the world yet a stranger to my being.

I believe my all is being used as a source of insurance,

making me liable for anything I think, do, or say out of context.

Therefore making me unreliable when it comes to on looking judgement.

What must I do to gain control of myself?

What badge of honor needs to be presented in order to gain my peace of mind,

that is only temporary?

so temporary that according to God I must suffer in order to appreciate it.

But after appreciation why can't there be indulgence.

If I could just keep it real for a moment.

My soul purpose for living is to reach eternity through death.

I understand that.

My head just can't seem to wrap itself around why can't there be heaven on earth?

Possibly further reading in my bible will justify those answers,

but where does application of those words lie?

A life unlived is no life at all.

Where is direction in a world of uncertainty?

I'll hold on to God's unchanging hand,

but what's to stop me from being pricked by a thorn everytime I see a rose bush.

Harmful yet thought-full.

Words-4-tha-Wise- Finding Direction In Life:

1. Figure out what you do not want to do with your life

2. Be honest about your capabilities and what you are willing to do

3. Take time to look at the stars/nature; relax

4. You are exactly where you are supposed to be

5. Set short term goals and gauge your satisfaction

6. Interview ten people who are doing what you would like to do

7. What do you already love to do for free

8. Block out time for creative thinking and/or meditation

9. Take action on one thing today

10. Go in the direction of fear and self doubt

Our Days

The time that I dedicate to myself is no more.

The floor needs to be cleaned,

and rid of selfish ways that stay in my mind.

Yet, I still find new things to want,

to fear,

yet hope that I will never fear,

a life in my hands.

On my life of which seeks perfection,

but no connection is made.

No shade to shield my eyes from the day's emotion.

Maybe some lotion to soften up my wrinkles,

soften the dry peaks upon my cheeks,

where my hips used to sway to the beat of a teenage soul.

Where my breast sat upon my chest,

and my figure was a vision of heaven at the age of seventeen.

But know there was also a smooth rhythm before my vision was lost,

yet not so lost just a little dusty.

My joints a little rusty in comparison to my days.

Yes, my days before the days of my children,

and maybe my children's children's days.

Of which I now cannot play as an individual,

because I stand for a population.

Now I am my mother and my mother's mother.

I have the weight of the universe on my shoulders.

Other People's Problems

I see the world in the eyes of my boy,

and my girls, they bring me so much joy,

and make my days seem well lived,

because now my days are their days;

and our lives are renewed,

until one day they see what I now view.

Words-4-tha-Wise- How To Age Gracefully:

1. Eat foods high in antioxidants

2. Stimulate your mind daily

3. Walk daily

4. Share meals with a friend/partner often

5. Change up a constant routine by adding tiny adjustments

6. Wear shoes that provide great arch support

7. Increase your intake of Omega-3 fatty acids

8. Dance often

9. Do exercises that promote strength, flexibility, and balance

10. Enjoy the honour of living a long life; May you be blessed by the generations that follow you

Beach and Bare

As I sit upon my pedestal

I want to fall freely among the crashing waves.

upon the shore

the door to my findings have not yet been found.

Yet upon walls of serenity,

I lie and dwell within my nudity.

Upon this rock I soar on clouds,

yet don't know how to make my emotions stop flowing;

stop glowing so life can go back to normal.

So my world won't seem so small.

No tears will come nor fall.

Be blank until the sun falls behind the mountain peak,

with a kiss upon my cheek from the sounds of whispers in my ear.

From the wind into my body

that lands upon my skin,

lies a bland canvas of purity.

Incongruity about my life confuses my hair and forces them to lie in the air instead of my face.

My shoulders which ages my skin and makes me grow older,

to feel free in a sea of blank time.

Words-4-tha-Wise- Fighting Emotional Numbness:

1. This state of mind is only temporary

2. Find out what the cause might be

3. Change the things that you can

4. Break up your routine every now and then

5. Surround yourself with people who are positive and energized

6. Relive all of your past joys

7. Focus on reigniting feelings of engagement and motivation

8. Pick one thing to pursue/invest your time in

9. Break down big projects into small measurable steps

10. Turn your small changes into habits

Fulfilled Emptiness

Since this becoming of a woman I've changed in ways,

and at times I feel as if my path has gone away.

For this becoming of a woman has mended my soul,

my body,

my mind,

my feet have grown cold.

I feel as if I'm on the outs hiding from what's within,

when in reality my fickle heart erases my grin.

To draw a frown upon my face for all the sorrow I feel,

then waking up every morning crying because I know what is real.

I no longer feel the warmth my people once had for me,

I feel ice upon my back while living in tragedy.

Other problems were simply solved ending in tears or possibly words,

but this problem of forsaken blessings has me speechless.

Its unheard of for things like this to occur with a girl like me.

possibly my womanhood was betrayed by masculinity.

This thing I cannot walk away from because I carry it wherever I go.

From my room, the streets, and my final blow.

No one shall ever know.

My embarrassment holds hands with my pity,

because I feel as if love has hit me low.

So low that I can't go to the people I know will throw everything to the side.

Tell me It's alright.

Let me know I have somewhere to run,

Other People's Problems

so I can build strength for the pain that has left me with shame,

and still try to have fun.

Never knew what these shoes would feel like until I walked through a field of grass.

staining the souls of which I walk on,

then falling right on my ass.

To find that I've hit rock bottom,

but only few remain to see that my secret is strong.

It haunts me while i'm awake,

even when I sleep.

See some problems come for a minute,

while others marinate to burn.

This problem will stay for a lifetime,

with pressures and lessons to learn.

My feet tired from walking on fire,

but they can't seem to find some rest.

yet I welcome gasoline and matches,

and pray that no problems will be met

I await with anxiety and pressure for the day I kill my all.

as if life was created for nothing,

to build just to watch it fall.

Words-4-tha-Wise- Overcoming Feelings of Emptiness:

1. Spend time with people you love and that love you back

2. Meet new people

3. Adopt a pet

4. Be kind to others

5. Explore why you may be feeling empty

6. Start journaling your thoughts and feelings

7. Understand that you may be depressed

8. Talk about your problems with a professional or someone you trust

9. If you have lost a loved one, you may still be grieving

10. Ask yourself if you have developed any addictions

A Different Mind

Upon my shoulders is where my bundle lies.

My no longer dry but wet eyes,

seem too common among these grounds.

No level of neutrality can be found.

No room for mistakes or proportion,

just a web of unclarity and distortion.

This life is worth living,

but what am I giving back.

One problem on top of another they stack.

Though my pile is high,

it's what I lack that exemplifies my cons;

my con-fusion,

my con-tacts,

my con-tracts,

my con-trol,

all of which seems to shy further away from my being,

as I continue down a road of uncertain destinations,

in depth but complex contemplations,

I seem to convince myself every once in awhile that I'm satisfied,

but yet I have yet to try something different.

So the alrights are then traded in for the why nots,

the I cans,

the I wish I was doing so much better than my better right now.

Situations can always be better,

Other People's Problems

but why not settle for less until the mess I've made comes clean.

So that all the things I once forsaked could come back,

so I may come back,

because it seems I've left the building for a little while.

When I try to smile there is nothing behind my grin,

there is no heart within my skin,

yet no room within myself to breath in.

The day her rashes went away my rashes had come to stay,

I feel as if my burden carries the weight of others' losses.

Therefore leaving me at a stand still,

because that is all I can do.

To stand still for nothing does not fulfill me anymore.

Nothing excites me anymore.

My thoughts consists of my mood rather than my dreams,

emotions are now only extreme,

and things are very different.

Things are not the same and I wish they were the same,

and now without,

I'm not sane,

and now without,

there is no one to blame,

and now without,

emptiness remains.

My chains are gone but I wish I was caged.

It wasn't so bad being tied down to earth,

Other People's Problems

now that I think about it,

It wasn't so bad having to answer to someone,

now that I think about it.

I am now free to go do/be whatever I please,

and it scares me to chills.

The thrill of being this person I thought I would be at this age is no longer the same.

Image trends, goals, and wants of my desire are now old,

instead of vintage.

Everything I thought I knew has left without a trace,

and now a blank look upon my face,

is what I share because I don't know where to regain my happiness,

with these things now missing.

I realize I really do care,

and it's really not fair,

that no one shares my fares,

I mean the price.

The cost of what was bought now broken,

what was said now unspoken,

the fruits of life no longer soak in.

I was used to the way things used to be,

now it seems the life I wanted has forsaken me,

a once caged ram is now set free,

left wondering when I am to expect my company.

Everything in my life has been stirred and shaken,

my passion for love has been taken,

and the first day of the rest of my life seems mistaken.

As if I have no life right now,

as if I wanted this somehow.

Words-4-tha-Wise- When You Realize You Want More Out of Life:

1. Tap into the confidence you were born with

2. Know your strengths and weaknesses

3. Expect success

4. Trust in your capabilities

5. Embrace the unknown

6. Take risks

7. Learn to receive praise

8. Practice confidence

9. Surround yourself with people who are doing what you love to do

10. Pursue your passions with passion

Dismissing Reality

A part of me doesn't seem to be too close to me anymore.

So sure I was once upon the right path,

so pure from rage and wrath,

so free from what really was.

My do's very rarely does what it's supposed to.

No longer close to,

what was my base.

No longer a smile upon my face.

The love within me I can no longer trace,

track down,

resolve,

not found.

Yet with all 132 pounds I chateau to a new high.

My love for faith, can make me fly,

but the high I once knew,

cannot be a part of my new life.

Which way do I go?

How am I supposed to know

what's good for me?

To just trust and see what happens,

but His ways will make things happen.

but where do I strap in my mind,

my soul,

my love my goals,

Other People's Problems

my courage, my drive,

my cool, my pride?

How do I conceal my anguish,

while maintaining my worship?

Do I no longer walk in light,

if my life doesn't go right?

Do I fight or strike back with the strength I forgot I had,

the force that made me glad,

glad to be me,

the me that loved to love and be loved in return.

To be let down and concerned,

yet bounce back and then learn,

but when does that step fall into play?

How do I acquire the role that I play?

How do I leave the place where I stay?

which I wish to be past tense,

Of which I hope I can fence,

out along with the loves of my past.

The struggles that never last.

The growth of which was once stunted,

the balls of life I once punted,

where lies and truths were once confronted.

I would like to receive the life I once wanted.

Things I seemed to find, moments in time.

Words-4-tha-Wise- When Dreams Don't Meet Expectations:

1. Understand the "why" behind your dreams

2. Do not become overwhelmed by trying to know all of the answers

3. Set measurable goals for yourself

4. Drop all exterior expectations

5. Do not fear success

6. Are you pursuing a dream or an impulse?

7. If you wouldn't mind quitting then it's probably not your passion

8. The change you may be experiencing is your mind becoming open to new things

9. You are not bored, you just require more of a challenge

10. How much of your time, money, and self are you willing to invest in order to reach your goals?

Cold

I paint pictures of the monsters that exist in my head,

for the world is cold outside my bedroom door.

I've been here before.

I noticed the foot print that I left as I walked away from here before.

I scurry off to new scenery,

repeating old history,

reliving new misery,

But not really.

I can only imagine the disdain and disorder that I present to the world,

for the world outside my head is biased.

The world doesn't cater to me so I scream away.

I fade away from what refuses to please me 100 percent.

From those who refuse to award the tears I've spent.

I lent my heart to a man then took it right back;

commitment means war of which I will always bite back,

and I mean that.

Well I meant that.

My stories gain their glory while I sit/eat/sleep/walk/think alone.

As I talk on the phone,

my tongue speaks lashings,

while my mind continues bashing the thought of love forever.

No vessel will trick me into ever having to stay.

But I'll play for a little while longer, ok.

I'll stay just a little while but eventually this pretty smile will walk away.

Other People's Problems

The statement "to stay" is no state meant for me,

visions of matrimony is no sight I can see,

but I see your face and I remember how it feels to say I love you.

How it feels to always get to wake up to your body heat.

Imperfection goes a long way.

Though here by my side,

my heart always hides from you,

finding reasons to not have to love you.

My cracks of insecurity sink deep,

Through my core to my feet,

so forgive me if I don't know how to keep my promises.

I shouldn't mean a thing to you,

heartache is what I will bring to you,

so leave me now before I leave you too.

<u>Words-4-tha-Wise- Facing Your Fear Of Commitment:</u>

1. Acknowledge that you have a fear

2. Find the courage to take risks anyway

3. Remain present

4. Learn from your past

5. Meditate when you sense fear

6. Don't put so much pressure on yourself

7. Before you run away, compare your pros and cons

8. Avoid over thinking

9. Understand that no relationship will be perfect

10. Discuss your fear with your partner

A Mother's Silence

She's silent when she has everything to say.

The clang of silence remains undisputed by Sex and the City,

as she sits,

and I sit in pitty,

of what we both want but don't have.

A loving husband and dad.

A relationship that never went bad.

Oh how I wish this list of worries were no longer my problem.

I am a young adult veteran living in restraint.

Yet no paint can cover the cold shoulder from a mother that loves beyond her own capacity.

Her tears are my fears as though I carry none of my own.

Her dreams bring me aspirations,

that share no relation with what I am currently going through.

Patience is breathe.

Therefore slow and left to think upon my own thoughts,

having all but nothing to say,

our silence is no longer awkward but familiar.

I remember when I used to run,

because I have never stopped running.

I have ran towards the corners of the earth to find wondrous works of the world.

Lives only commonly lived on the pages of travel and dreams.

I have found all destinations,

all novel experience and impartations,

Other People's Problems

all of everything short of myself.

God guide me.

Lord please provide for me a way to become myself that is pleasing in your eyes.

Give me the strength to dig past these breasts and thighs.

Help me to lead a life that gains the approval of my mother's wise intentions.

Why am I not good enough?

Why do I still feel inadequate?

Where is the fullness of myself that quenches the mental starvation of a lifetime?

Why have all my friends become distant pin pals?

Why are the loves of my life incrementing my time and space,

In what seems to take the place of what love should be?.

Why is there love not good enough for me?

Am I not loving myself enough for me?

Why am I not the boss of me?

I don't like the way I've been living.

Can't seem to appreciate the blessings I've been given,

And every other moment of the day my painful past is reliving in me.

My old days and cold ways are way too close to me.

When will I ever be free?

I tasted freedom once,

and it was bliss to know,

That the mist would show up on my cheeks in the middle of morning dew.

I almost forgot what myself felt like.

Other People's Problems

Because my mind and eyes were always closed just tight enough to never feel the freedom of a full beautiful day.

The sun outside my window never had quite enough light to spackle a smile upon my face.

Why am I/was I running another mans race?

I am now forced to embrace the tear stains on my face,

freckled in disdain in order to retrain my heart.

To stop living to fulfill neighboring shoe visions of success that were never meant for my feet.

To say what I mean and stand by what I speak.

Stop trying to be so sweet.

To busy people pleasing.

To preoccupied feeding into pumped up news feeds of,

trumped up chances,

of unlived lives.

Tattered hearts and tampered dreams do not destroy ambition,

they tailor vision.

They create wisdom.

I can no longer be numb to my dumb decisions.

My poor choices.

I should not ignore the voices in my head that tell me to get out of that man's bed,

and back into my own life.

I am more than some foolish man's future ex-wife.

Nights stained in Japanese cherry blossoms and pink ice,

cause me to think twice on falling back into a pattern once drawn.

I was never meant to play the pawn in my own life.

Other People's Problems

But this is how it always starts.

This is usually the part where my emotions tweak my nerves.

Where my actions never match my words.

Where I am time and time again reminded of my should haves,

where I should have listened to myself,

but this time I'd rather not.

I want to actually receive what I've been taught,

instead of being broken and caught up.

Please forgive my lies,

and accept my tries and attempts to be a better me.

And if not please know that it was not your acceptance that was being sought,

but my freedom being bought.

So do please forgive me,

Or not.

Words-4-tha-Wise- Becoming A Better Decision Maker For Your Life:

1. Make all important decisions in the morning

2. Increase your glucose intake (refer to a medical professional)

3. Create a schedule to conserve your energy for extra decisions

4. Make time for sleep, healthy eating, and excercise

5. Increase your interaction with a respected influence

6. Take time to sleep or think on situations

7. Refer to your close network for limited advice

8. Don't beat yourself up for saying yes to wrong decisions

9. You do not always have to decide

10. The best decision makers know when not to trust themselves

Not Use To the "Over"

Please forgive me as I try to remember that you are no longer my man.

Doors you'll no longer open for me,

phone calls will cease to ring abundantly,

you no longer have time for me any more.

So now as I dwell on my issues with romance,

I will relive every lived out performance of the time we used to share.

Please excuse the fact that I still care about you.

I'll try to be discreet every time I check up on you.

I'm just having a hard time believing that my dreams of you are now over;

even in October when our paths were slowly departed.

I will never forget how the union of we started.

I will try to remember my temper when I think of I how I started what seems to be every argument,

how I debated our love as though it was parliament,

but none of that even matters anymore,

you forgot to leave my heart on the counter as you left.

Our good times you kept,

and now I'm left with sad memories of how in love we used to be.

For now I will leave your number in the archives of my phone.

So that one day while I'm home alone,

I will stomach the courage to call.

Just to say that I was wrong.

I was wrong for believing you should be perfect,

and wrong for acting as though you were never worth my time.

I was wrong for acting ashamed and treating you like you were never mine.

Other People's Problems

I hate the fact that I never chose your side in my head.

I now remember how long and cold the nights would feel in our bed

as we lied in secret.

So far and separated from our love.

My heart would feel renovated from a single hug from you.

Make up kisses reminded me of becoming Mrs Green.

I apologize for how I let my attitude come between us.

And I cannot stomach the fact that your heart can no longer see us in the distance.

My memories of you are proof of your existence in my happiness.

However our awkward nights remind me of the emptiness we both shared.

My heart was never prepared to share you.

I hate that you never cared to take long walks with me,

or share long talks with me,

you just preferred the simple thought of me.

I'm sorry you ever got caught up in me.

I have too much of your stuff with me.

Please pick it up so that I can get back to me.

My heart mourns the misprint of our relation,

and with no need of heavy interpretation,

I still love you like nights and movies.

Like morning bus rides with you trying to pursue me.

I will still love you when love is no longer allowed,

and until then I will always search for your face in the crowd.

Words-4-tha-Wise- Letting Go of Your X:

1. Take some time to be sad

2. Keep reminders of them out of sight and out of mind

3. Talk your problems out with your friends

4. Do something you've been wanting to do

5. Rearrange your space

6. Pamper/treat yourself

7. Work Out

8. Learn something new

9. Read books

10. Have fun

Hello Everyone

I cannot begin to believe that I do not care about how I make others feel,

so forgive me if I become uneasy around the pain of others tears.

My purpose isn't to scold the unkept, the poor,

nor the heavy and light hearted.

I do not believe in keeping it 1-hunnit,

no man has ever done it.

There is no such thing as complete honesty.

Our brains don't work at full capacity,

and our eyes fill in gaps that our mind cannot perceive,

so how can you fully comprehend what you cannot completely receive.

I refuse to give up on my dreams of true love,

to simply shrug off the existence of gentle words from gentlemen,

because mental men never knew how to treat me.

You are a theory and theoretically if I do this,

Then you will do that .

Then we will build this on top of that,

but what I think does not necessarily equate fact.

I am merely surviving the struggle of high self -esteem;

and please do tell me what it means,

to be pretty for a dark girl.

Don't worry,

I'll wait.

Or let's revisit my short curls.

I guess that's in these days.

Other People's Problems

But there is no easy way to let go of everything you ever knew to be beautiful about you.

I had to find beauty in me.

I have to constantly remind myself that,

we don't have to like each other,

we don't have to be together,

I don't have to look like her,

and we don't have to speak to understand each other,

I heard you.

I love my mother;

she is my laughter in hard times,

and warmth in cold weather.

I adore my father;

he gave me beauty when I didn't see it,

and gave me the world telling me to always expect it,

and accept nothing less.

Drinking had a problem with me.

I broke up with my best friend be because she,

was different.

I hate the lie that I tell every time I don't answer the phone,

acting as though I'm not home when I really just don't feel like talking to you.

Early mornings give me headaches,

I guess I'll never grow out of heartbreaks,

and the food I love gives me heartburn.

I am so ready to be rich right now.

Other People's Problems

I don't know how to be ok with negative criticism.

Who are you to think I am not correct and amazing.

I buy way too many clothes,

but I never have anything to wear,

I guess I'm allergic to alphet repetition,

as if my mission in life is to wear everything I own once,

then banish it from my life.

I will never be a wife.

At least that's what one of my Ex's said.

Because you see I never cook,

I can read my ass off though,

all because someone said if you don't want black people to know it,

put it in a book.

I'm on my way to reading all of their secrets.

I live an alternative lifestyle;

I'm single with secrets.

I have multiple ratchet tendencies,

but I'm qualified to be a Queen.

I just love thrill of how the other half lives,

but don't worry you can trust me,

I'm clean.

And for all of you who don't know,

Weed and I are no longer together.

So stop bringing him up.

I no longer drink wine to ease my mind,

Other People's Problems

my future good habits will be my turn up.

Dear random guy,

no we cannot be friends,

no you can't have my number,

and I'm busy every weekend.

Dear perfect man,

I know I don't deserve you right now,

so could you vacation from my thoughts so that I can appreciate a life without true love for now.

Dear God,

Please forgive me.

Disobedient is not something I would try to be I'm just working through some insecurities.

Dear world,

I will not kill myself trying to understand you,

but you are as beautiful as the nights are long,

and as terrifying as my first kiss.

Dear me,

always remember to take care of me,

always be prepared to love me,

through bad times and weight gain.

Remember nothing lasts always,

and never forsake daydreams,

and move past the fear that leers in the deeper end of the pool.

Even when it gets hard make sure you stay in school,

grab a hold to your life and ignore what you may lack,

and always remember to always love hard,

regardless of whether love will hug you back.

Words-4-tha-Wise- Accepting Yourself As You Are:

1. Set positive intentions for yourself

2. Acknowledge that you have strength and talent

3. Spend time with people who positively influence your life

4. Surround yourself with people who accept and believe in you

5. Free yourself from past regret through forgiveness

6. Ignore your negative self talk

7. Write down all of your thoughts, ideas, and dreams

8. Always give to others when the opportunity presents itself

9. Speak to the highest version of yourself

10. Be kind to yourself

I Write

The next time I am cornered by someone who asks me what is it that I do with my life,

I will unapologetically respond that I write.

And if in any case you should feel misunderstood,

relax and know that I am good and good at it.

Please know that my flow does not require practice,

for this is God's gift that has been bestowed upon me.

And no I do not necessarily write for a living;

I write to keep living.

I write so that I can keep giving to the world what muses my intrigue.

My fingers never grow tired from fatigue,

because my words are a means to my beginnings.

My lyrics are the cost of my living.

And for every time I ever felt tempted to excuse my lack of career,

please know that I am sincere when I say that my poetry makes me happy!

I illuminate every time someone facilitates emotions that I must describe.

My words they,

they make me come alive!

It is a feeling that I cannot describe.

If I had to do this for the rest of my life,

I would die happily tomorrow knowing that my pen gave me life;

that my notepad was my greatest gift;

that somehow one word that I wrote somehow would uplift

one soul.

Clarity has made it clear that I now have one goal;

Other People's Problems

To be Thee Prolific Poet!

Now I know the answer to my life's meaning.

Knowing your purpose can feel redeeming,

when you've lived your life according to someone else's list of accomplishments.

"I loved your poem" was the day I received my favorite compliment.

It loved you too.

I no longer write for just me,

I now write for you!

I write for those who have foes and sit quietly.

I write for those who feel alone,

you can share this home with me.

I write for zip tied lips,

you no longer have to hurt silently.

I write for you the one who claims to need therapy.

I write to say whatever the hell I think I feel,

and when I speak those words to you,

My world in your life somehow becomes real.

I write because I talk too much and I need somebody to talk to,

To flow through,

To grow to.

So know you are never alone.

If you ever need someone to talk to,

download my poetry to your cell phone.

My wisdom and words shall build my dream home.

Other People's Problems

So never fear pursuing your happiness for the sake of status or relationships.

Hone your craft to feel the only sense of accomplishment.

You will grow farther,

you will work harder,

and you will live today as if everyday was recess.

Put down the expectations that you didn't meet on your IQ test.

Make life matter to you and never regress.

Create without protest,

and go home every night knowing you always did your best.

Leave the rest,

to those who are still sleeping.

I cherish the day that I started living instead of dreaming!

Live the life you love,

Or spend the rest of every day fantasizing about what could've -- Been.

<u>Words-4-tha-Wise- How to Pursue Your Passion:</u>

1. Ask yourself what you want from life

2. What do you need in order to get what you want

3. Figure out which part of the day you are the most productive

4. Place yourself into a supportive environment

5. Show gratitude and appreciation towards your day job

6. Start your own personal project

7. Research things that bring you joy

8. Ask yourself how you can help solve a problem for someone else

9. Be patient

10. Never give up on your dream

Broke and Broken

Dreams shatter when your pockets can't seem to fathom the extent of your potential.

Hearts chatter at the thought of being broken in one more place,

because you have now allowed time and space for hurt and pain to exist.

Resist feeling helpless,

and no,

the answer is not to become selfish.

Just remember yourself and your purpose.

Obstacles and opposing ideals sometimes feels like the beginning of an end,

because there is no real mending of the pieces.

There is no real testing of this thesis,

because the mind has now grown tired.

Acceptance of a normal life has been retired from your thoughts,

and you are now failing into your independence.

There are no rooms for worries or repentance,

because you are not finished making a mess,

so instead of waking up every day to get dressed you stay in bed,

and rethink every dollar you shed.

Remember when you said that your dreams were worth reaching.

Remember when someone else said that failure was the initial beating you receive,

and the teaching you believe to have been wasted,

has now been tasted by virgin fingertips.

Everything that was wrong to do now belongs to you,

Other People's Problems

as if a transacted secret where only you and the universe could have predicted.

Now your goals that were once scripted have been redrafted.

Details are now compacted into each word.

You no longer only take action on just things that you've heard,

your instinct inspires you to research.

So you don't feel hurt from making the same mistake in the same way.

I wish that all my tomorrows would learn from how I fucked up yesterday.

Mistakes I meant to do over,

I now only have the choice to move over,

and make up for what my mind wasn't able to make out yesterday.

Remaining boggled over problems only means you have no solutions,

and those very toxins and pollutions will block you from your goals.

And no,

you may never know when your someday is coming,

but if you're headed in the right direction,

I suggest you start running.

Words-4-tha-Wise- How To Cope While Broke On Your Way To Success:

1. Meditate on financial mistakes that you have made in the past

2. Find a part time job that is related to your passion

3. Get in touch with 3 successful friends/family members

4. Sign up for one free networking event per month

5. Read 10 books in the field of your passion

6. Cut expenses that are not mandatory

7. Create something that you can duplicate and sell/market

8. Be willing to adapt to new changes and new environments

9. Take a free class on managing finances

10. Find a mentor that will help you work smarter, not harder

My Friends Call Me Fluffy

Controls are what keep me from saying how I really feel,

as if me telling you what is really real will harm you.

My demeanor was not meant to alarm you.

I'm simply satisfied seeking no offense in common conversation.

I sometimes like to harp on my opinion as though my heart and intuition know what it is that is best for you.

So instead of leaving a mess for you to clean up,

I will adjust the tone of my voice,

so that my choice words make you feel as if my contributions,

are simply helpful additions that presume you need no change,

while "how you can change your life slowly settles in."

I was met with a compliment and a cheerful grin,

when a woman called me beautiful but believed I was suppose to be bald.

My gratuitous smile saw right through it all,

but she left me to feel beautifully incomplete.

Forcing me to compose new music on a different sheet of paper.

Still lovely at conception,

but it will just take a second to pull together the connection,

that reminds me that I am still beautiful.

I told a woman with endless problems that she was perfect the way she was,

and that remaining yourself never does anything but make sense.

I spoke with high hopes of tearing down the fence that guards her ability to feel happy and loved.

With heartfelt and securely gloved context.

Other People's Problems

You are the after math or what comes next in your own life.

You need to feel that you are the beautiful disposition to your own sight.

In this life there will never be comparisons for you potential.

You are the prototype the floor model and the example,

stop handing out hate simply because your plate was never filled by someone else.

I told a man once that he was my superman and that no love from another man could deter me.

I told him that I knew his love would always prefer me,

and that his methods on how he chooses to love does not concern me.

You can only truly show love if you truly love yourself,

and I'm sure you don't need my help,

but I'll always be there to remind you that you are wonderful.

Your timing and tactics always seem to keep me full of how much more of myself I'd be willing to give you.

You must be able to live through light.

Insightful incentive is the key to loving yourself into happiness.

Where the elevation of one's thoughts about oneself makes perfect sense,

and thoughts of living without compliments,

brings about discerning discontent.

Don't live in a world full of words that make you feel wrong.

It's not mandatory that you belong In a constant state of depression.

Lovingly made confessions to your own heart will start the evolution of a more confident you.

Where you alone can choose to stay that way.

A hurtful critique doesn't always have to feel that way.

Be positive to negative people so they don't have words to say.

Other People's Problems

Cancel out their ammunition,

to be kindly correct is your ambition.

Don't be easily swayed by predators who have made the decision to hate you,

simply because they were made without love,

never received a decent hug,

and can hardly recognize the term to live above.

Don't feel shoved into petty participations,

or feel enclosed by dysfunctional relations,

that leave you feeling resentful.

Be willing to wonder what life actually looks like through rose colored glasses.

Don't be overly concerned with what you don't have and the world of perfect asses.

Those seeking to steal your thunder are classless,

and happen to have less of themselves.

Find power in pointing out the glorious.

Speak with optimism so that those that receive your energy will become victorious.

You have the right to love yourself into succession,

be precious with your love so that you may leave behind perfect first impressions.

Impress upon yourself to always speak light and love into yourself.

Leave speculators speechless over the sparkle of your wealth.

Words-4-tha-Wise- How To Not Look For Outside Validation:

1. Your opinion of yourself is the only opinion that matters

2. Remaining silent is a great way to let go of things we hear

3. View your insecurities as challenges you have to overcome

4. Do not change who you are/what you do in order to be liked

5. Don't let others convince you of what they believe you should care about

6. Go on a social media diet every now and then

7. Do not engage in forced interactions

8. Let go of the urge to constantly people please

9. Spend more time getting to know yourself

10. Learn to accept others for who they are

When Your Spirit is Under Attack

There is plenty of evidence of hatred a foot.

You will offer them inches and they will steal an extra foot.

Pay attention to the way they look at you.

They will smile in your face while looking down at you.

Laughing with their friends after they just cried with you.

Come hug and kiss your face after they've lied to you.

Ask you for so much help till they have everything.

Turn around then sit and watch you be broke and won't say anything.

Will seem convincing with their concern and it won't mean a thing.

Go so far as to pawn your mother's wedding ring.

Rode with you everywhere you would go,

but now that you're hurting they act like they don't know how to find you anymore.

This is not what friendships are for.

You'll run low on energy and they'll selfishly want more.

Fake friends turn into chores.

The last time turns into four more.

Significant others aren't even sure that they still want you.

They will use and abuse and then flaunt you.

You deserve to be held onto by something solid.

To be fondly remembered not just whatyoucallit.

What happened to the help that we all said that we needed.

Follow the lord in this life you will need him.

Don't you continue to feed him if that means one more brick on your plate.

Let go of that dad who won't even opt to be late,

Other People's Problems

He just never shows.

You look so much like him but don't even know,

Where building better relationships meets I can no longer take this shyt!

I can no longer fake and sit and act like all of those wrongs will be ok in the end.

When you have morals don't let anyone bend you into distorted decisions

especially when you already knew that your open trust would build your prison.

And those who claim to love you helped you lay every brick,

now you're angry, unhealthy, unhappy, and sick because,

they drained all of your light.

The evil will prey on those who do right.

Stop giving absolutes to those who can only promise they might.

For yourself you must always fight!

Words-4-tha-Wise- Letting go of toxic relationships:

1. Stop living in denial about people in your life who make you feel bad or drain your energy

2. Take time to be alone in order to heal

3. Don't lose hope for your future happiness

4. Stay connected to positive people and environments

5. Gain an understanding of why you entered and stayed in a toxic relationship

6. Work on rebuilding your confidence and self-esteem

7. Declutter your space and rearrange furniture in your home

8. Think back on the strength that helped you get out of other relationships

9. Choose to follow your brain and not your heart

10. Do not keep in touch

<u>When love</u>

What exactly am I supposed to do when my love begs me for forever?

Even though I never allow him to be at peace.

He lubricates his mouth as if he's going to grease my scalp,

but at least he says he loves me.

Maybe one day I'll love the way we fight.

Maybe I love it now.

Maybe I'll never know how to to not be broken;

to not be jealous.

Maybe one day people will tell us that our love was meant to exist.

Maybe every forehead kiss was intentional.

Maybe every stroke of bliss was meant to give my mind a kiss every time I thought I would miss you.

I pray I never forget to feed you compliments,

acknowledge every accomplishment,

and rub every tension,

so that moments like this stay worth mentioning.

Phone calls in the dark next to the love of your life,

will plant the seed for the very next fight that is about to come.

Every argument will fuck you until you're about to come,

and you'll never be done with this man.

He will hold your hand in public places.

Wipe all the smiles off you worried friends faces.

He will be the reason why you know that 6000 paces = 3 miles,

for you dropped a tear through every step.

Wondering why you didn't ring his neck when you had the chance to.

Other People's Problems

He's so disrespectful,

but honestly he's not even a bad dude.

He can be a bit rude if I give him some of this attitude.

But I need him to endure my every mood.

Not just because Disney promised me a happily ever after,

but because you were so cute when you approached me after the day party.

You looked as though you planned to love me hardly,

and not like not hardly but the kind of hard that graduates to ly.

Trips to the coast that fed my glee.

The reason why tv is just our background noise.

He creates feelings in me that I cannot avoid.

But I digress.

I love being undressed in your company.

And he loves that I like that that's what he expects from me.

I get carried away with being his freak.

Every hug leaves me unplugged.

His absence gives me withdraws,

and I don't think I've ever missed one of his calls,

because I anticipate his curiosity,

and I think it's cute when he's the boss of me.

Except on days when I do what I want,

and he hates that I flaunt the fact that I'm free.

Like free means me away from he.

Free just means I'm free to be an indulger.

Free like waking me up to a can of folgers,

Other People's Problems

because I can't wait to get up and look at you.

Now I'm mad, but I still love to look at you.

I say it's over but my eyes yearn to see what your heart will do.

How many me-less nights are you willing to live through?

How many hearts have to break before there is finally a breakthrough?

I choose you.

And not just simply because you chose me,

but I want this relationship simply because I feel like it,

and I will break up with you a million times before I ever dare to really try it.

I like him with me because that's the way I like it;

even when I don't like him.

My yes' never seem to make sense,

because a minute ago when I spoke of you in past tense,

you believed that I wanted you to go.

But you also always let me know,

that you never plan to go anywhere.

I dream of making love to you everywhere.

I even smile while I'm folding his underwear.

But I hope you never tare me again,

because my feelings won't lie or pretend as if there won't be an attempt to cut you,

but you already know that I will always love you.

Words-4-tha-Wise- How To Deal With Being Cheated On:

1. Express how you truly feel with someone you trust

2. Do not avoid the emotional weight of the pain you are feeling; you will grow stronger

3. Cry so that you can heal

4. Someone's lack of ability to remain faithful is not your problem to solve

5. A change in relationship status may be scary but also may be necessary for your peace of mind

6. Do not become vengeful; tackle your pain with peace

7. Listen to music that makes you feel strong

8. Surround yourself with friends and family who love you and want to make you smile/laugh (I believe that laughter heals broken hearts)

9. Understand that this time in your life is temporary

10. Lies only exist where they are welcome

Crimson Legacy

Menstrual cycling through life on the cotton pony;

Here's to catching every drop.

You make my heart stop when you're late,

and when you're early you interrupt first dates.

I turn down dinner plates at the thought of my grumbling stomach pains.

Blissful lazy days spent cocooned around my aquarian bottles that bring forth warmth once warmed in the heater.

You're more than a faithful fever that's washed away by sudafeds and Vix.

You my dear are the reason why caffeine and cramps don't mix;

why broken hymans cannot be fixed,

and by the fruits of life that explain why we still exist.

Beautifully abrasive you make me a woman in my most natural form.

Vulnerable and in need of companionship,

an enticing peaceful and sweet man reminds the blood that's flowing through me that we are relational.

The psychological effect of standing by 4th of July windows somewhere after my 12th birthday.

You introduced me to modesty.

Keep your vagina clean,

tuck the vagina in on bloody days so that her alarmist ways don't distract neighboring eyes.

No longer can you lie about virginities and charities of the overwhelmed heart.

Your very construction divinely crafts the production of beautiful faces.

Yet within your warm embraces you cause others to walk lightly and in fear of the hormonal bitch on her period.

By the way ladies,

101

Other People's Problems

never date a man that's grossed out by your period.

That's like loving women without stretch marks.

Simply made men don't understand the wonders that make you woman.

My period is beautiful,

sometimes she's terrible,

but she breaks me down and cleanses the pathway to life.

To the cooker of life!

You live in me;

loved as mother-in-laws,

where her visits are displeasing,

because her presence involves the ceasing and halting of all things on your schedule.

Your painful love taps are searing and perpetual.

But you ease into the end as if a treasured friend were leaving after a weekend well spent.

You were meant to come again.

Reminding you and the self within,

that for now I will always come back to you.

I'm hear to remind you that you are beautiful,

through sore breasts,

and inflated waistlines,

you are the only factor that creates timelines.

You are ever present and unforgiving,

and while you're gone I'll commence to living normally.

When I'm gone there will never be more of me.

Though my flow may be unruly yet lawful;

Other People's Problems

I won't commit to always feeling awful when she comes around.

I wanna go dancing and swimming like the girls in the commercials.

Like the ones where girls on their rag run through parks and flip in circles.

My period is an ongoing biological life light.

She's the key that attaches me to my own birthright,

and I'm so glad my last day was last night!

Turn off the flashlight.

Words-4-tha-Wise- How To Get Through Your Period With The Least Pain and Inconvenience Possible:

1. Stay hydrated before, during, and after

2. Use heat to relax stomach cramping

3. Eat less (or completely cut out) meat and dairy

4. Engage in physical activity

5. Keep track of your cycle to help prevent surprises

6. Resist excessive (or any) drug intake

7. Treat yourself to something you enjoy during this time

8. Change out your pad and tampons frequently throughout the day

9. Take warm baths

10. Take this time to allow your body to rest if needed

I Can't Love You

Hey first I just want to say that I do care about you,

your day,

and whether or not you're having a good one.

But I do have a few things to say.

Pretty much things you've often heard me say before,

and I hate that I can't bring myself to say things like this to you in person.

But it never ends well for me when we try to have productive conversations about our relationship.

The truth is I don't want to be in a relationship anymore.

I don't hate you,

and even though you do things I don't like that's not it either.

Taking that space the other day was hard for me to do but also very necessary.

I really don't know how to explain it,

but I would just like all of my space back.

I never take the time to just be single and work things out that are going on with me,

and it doesn't make it better when I just pile how I feel on top of you when you already have enough to be worried about.

Lately I've been distant because I just don't trust,

and this is deeper than trying to work things out with you.

I just need to work things out for myself.

I know I always say this and I always upset you when I bring it up,

But I never enforce it because I don't want to miss out on you or this relationship.

I know you say things will get better,

105

Other People's Problems

But before we get better I have to get better.

I may be cocky and a little selfish but I've spent my whole life assisting/ being there for/going to check on/letting somebody stay with me,

and I'm just tired of always taking care of someone else,

or caring about how I'm going to make someone else feel over how I truly feel.

It may be selfish and one sided to you,

but my side needs to be good before I can even think of trying to be good for you or anyone else.

I would just stay in the relationship and wait for things to get better but I feel like that's just me putting off the inevitable.

I'll understand if you don't want to deal with me outside of a relationship,

but I hope you understand that I have to do what's best for me while I still can.

I don't want to stay in this relationship unhappy leaving you the impression that things are fine,

But all in all I would like to break up and I would like you to move out.

You no longer owe me my happiness.

I love you and I pray that you take away more understanding than anger.

Words-4-tha-Wise- How To Break Up With Someone and Mean It:

1. Surround yourself with people who love you

2. Spend more time by yourself

3. Consider having a friendly intervention from people you trust

4. Do not ignore your gut feeling

5. Do not drag out your decision

6. Focus on growth not faults

7. Do not feel guilty for feeling bad

8. Spend even more time with friends and family who love you

9. Be honest but not harsh

10. Know that tough decisions are always hard to make

Bad Sex

I'm sorry to break all of your lil fragile egos,

but men I need you all to know,

that you can no longer simply just beat it.

Our sexual needs have been mistreated.

We have clits and tits that navigate where some attention is also needed.

I'm the type of woman who treasures caresses.

Not the pounding of your groin as it presses into me.

I need you to sex me intimately.

I need you to have sex with me entirely.

Just start with the way you look at me.

I know you're anxious for us to feel how big you can be,

but remember that we'll get there soon enough,

and that doesn't mean I don't like it rough;

I just like it right!

I like sex at night,

I love love making with dim lights.

I love soft music in the background,

It makes it so much easier for you to go back round.

Kissing my shoulders will show that now you have found me.

Remember to lick and kiss all around me,

and never forget to go down town.

Don't be low down-- Reciprocate!

So that at least while we fornicate I can reach a proper climax.

Creative grinding and pounding won't make me do that.

Other People's Problems

And oh yea Never ever spit on me;

you need me to get a little wetter,

then go back to step 1 where I said to kiss on me.

And don't simply pull me into your shoulder because you came and now you think it's over.

How about you retrace your steps and never let me let go of the sensation.

It takes us longer to cum because most women use concentration,

and that's why masturbation might follow up most of your performances.

We love you dearly but we biologically need more than this.

That's also why most women prefer another woman over men.

We are tired of trying to mend your shattered confidence,

when I'm simply trying to lead you to an accomplishment,

that will let us know your giving us your best.

Forget about the rest,

stop listening to friends with all that mess,

they've never made their girl cum either.

Your girl can cum in three ways and she's experienced neither.

Unless you want batteries or Jeffrey's to be your permanent replacement,

Start paying attention to proper body placement.

Become one with us we need your engagement.

We have sex for quality,

we're not some skeez that you fuck in the basement.

Your becoming complacent,

and I just thought I'd be the one to let you know,

because women get together and we talk about the things you'll never know, like how you tried really hard and we don't want to hurt your feelings,

so we clench our kegels on demand and fake climax to protect your feelings.

It's your pride that were feeding.

Or how about all of the times we've never been close.

You make us chuckle with all those crazy positions,

but yet "am I ready to cum?" -- NO!!!

"Do we like it when you bite our nipples too hard?" -- NO!!!

"Is it ok to suck on the clit too hard?" -- NO!!!

"It might be ok to put in our ass, but, GO SLOW!!!

What the fuck do you think is happening?

That part of our body doesn't have proper elasticity,

and don't use so much tongue when you're kissing me.

Wet mouth is disgusting get off of me.

Remember to wash your dick and balls properly.

So that my vagina doesn't have to start acting improperly.

And yes I want to use fucking protection,

so that nine months from now when I become a part of your neglections,

I won't have a child who looks like your reflection,

or better yet catch a sexually transmitted infection,

just because you want me feel the skin on your erection.

And if you plan to sex us then not text us prevent yourself from vexing us, and just don't.

Now if your stamina is a bit sub par,

go to the gym instead of the bar,

and no I won't suck your dick while you're driving this car,

Other People's Problems

because it's stupid!

Don't act like it was Cupid who sent you to me.

It was my pretty ass and face that made you pursue me,

and now you can't even do me how I want to be done.

Do you know how terrible sex becomes when you never get to cum?

I just wanted share a little on where most of us might be coming from.

And I know you probably think I'm not talking to you,

but you see your girl was at the meeting too,

so guess what sir this poem is also for you too.

So now that you know better,

do better.

Or the day will come soon when she runs into Trevor,

and Trevor, he never misses.

Trevor can grant all sexual wishes.

Very specific with all of his kisses.

You know the kind of man that can make you cum,

squirt,

cook breakfast,

and wash the dishes.

if I could could grant three wishes for all the women in the house tonight,

I would make sure every touch made you feel just right,

I would grant you great sleep and great dick at night,

and make every stroke so orgasmic that you loose all your sight;

Now men get it right!

Words-4-tha-Wise- How To Make A Bad Sex Life Great:

1. You may be involved with the wrong person

2. Increase your level of sensitivity towards your partner and their needs

3. Talk about things you may be scared or nervous to do in bed with your partner

4. Understand that everyone has different definitions of pleasure

5. Sex is a craft that will grow with experience

6. Work on understanding or easing your partner's mood before attempting to start

7. There must be some source of general attraction before sexual acts take place

8. Communicate outside of the bedroom about questions and concerns you truly have about your sex life

9. Great sex can only occur when there is a deep level of mental intimacy

10. Only pursue a sexual act when both parties are willing and able

Foresight

If my future does not belong to me,

it is because I have put others in charge of me.

It is because I fear what's to become of me.

It is because I have neglected the responsibility of taking care of me.

If you ask me about my tomorrows,

I will show you all of the dreams that I borrowed.

Words-4-tha-Wise- How To Think For Yourself:

1. Seek out the answers to your own questions

2. Forced opinions from others do not have to be accepted

3. Be ok with disagreeing with people

4. You do not have to convince others to believe in your point of view

5. Ask yourself frequently what it is that you want or want to do

6. Do not make it a point to be a know it all

7. Remain humble

8. Live outside of your comfort zone

9. Understand that thinking for yourself comes with the full responsibility of your words/actions

10. Do not fear the possibility of being wrong

Problems

Past due phone bills with a side of menstrual cramp pills,

right next to the dinner bill on the table.

My man ain't actin' right.

these fucking jeans are too tight.

will I ever live my life right according to the word?

Mothers always know how to do something better.

I'm sick and tired and not getting better.

That nigga never even read my letter.

My boss is mean and I'm a part of a team that I really don't care to be on.

And because my boyfriend likes it raw but forgot to pull out,

I now have a stick I have to pee on.

I wish I had some bullshyt-be-gone.

Surrounded by items I could never afford,

But credit card limits forced my impulse to explore.

Now my back is sore because I have to drive Lyft to kill the difference.

I gave too much money when when someone else's pockets were funny.

I hate San Diego when it's not bright and sunny.

Red meat hurts my tummy,

but the poison is so addicting.

I have experienced bouts with brokenness.

Acting like I'm not one foot away from homelessness.

All because I failed to live how I was predicting.

I sit and think on my bed alone,

how thousands at a time were taken from my own only to water the air that's in front of me.

Other People's Problems

I still eat out too much.

I don't cook so dating men sucks,

because they all expect you to cook for them.

My landlord is a foreign misogynist.

I don't really think I was cut out for colleges,

and my very long list of accomplishments have only gained me
compliments.

Compliments won't pay for the house that I said I would have one day.

I refuse to change because I feel I was made this way.

But I guess the world is upset by conceit.

I really wish I was a tiny bit neat.

And half the people that I greet on the street don't even speak back.

Baby mothers are the bane of my existence.

2 months ago I was tryna lose weight.

My body changed and now my weight is losing itself.

Causing others to question my health,

as if anyone ever felt better after you told them they looked tired.

I plan to retire by the time I'm 30,

and that's if my dreams don't fire me or consider me unworthy.

I am worthy of better everything.

I guess I'll never know the weight of a wedding ring.

Always tempted by places saying they're hiring,

because somehow the money means more than the desiring.

I desire to live in comfort,

but I guess the world feels that I'm lazy and not concerned.

Other People's Problems

I just want to relearn the chapter in biology that said that every man is a scientist.

I wish to lose all my breaths through novel experience.

I choose to reside on cloud 9 and I'm serious.

Someone said my period would go away if I become vegan.

But red meat is so good I can't even begin.

I guess I'll take another 800 milligrams of that Motrin,

to even out these cramps and Hennessy potions,

and I just ran out of my favorite lotion.

Damn!

Words-4-tha-Wise- Embracing Optimism:

1. Always expect greatness in everything

2. Take action on the things that are in your control, let go of the things that are not

3. Stay around positive people, places, and information

4. Write positive affirmations on something that you look at everyday

5. Make plans (business/vacation)

6. Celebrate every single accomplishment

7. Create positive mantras in your life

8. Focus on your success

9. Don't try to predict the future

10. Show gratitude towards everything

Unanswered Questions

How can you begin to inspire others when your very own covers are covered in the same lies they tell themselves?

When you constantly lie to yourself as well.

Why is it that I never seem to get well?

I sure seem to get over.

I'll climb over,

speak over,

even bend over,

if it means I get one more smile.

How do I show others how to practice working it out when I can't even get out of my own relationships.

Hashtag "niggas ain't shit" has become my recreationship.

I seem to always miss the mark.

I feel so pretty but yet it's hard to ever feel exceptional,

When my love life is always the subject of confessional.

I am a professional at falling in love.

And the word fall should have warned me of danger.

But I saw "go" where it said "slow" and now I have adopted another stranger.

Another ranger over my do's and don'ts.

That comes with a list of the things that he'll do and he won't.

Somehow I always knew that my future would say don't.

Do not see pot then unblock that nigga,

because he comes with amenities.

He'll sugar you up then spit you out as though you were always his worst enemy,

Other People's Problems

he used to be a friend to me.

Use to call me sweet and friendly,

now all you do is fucking pretend to be my rock.

There is nothing hard about you.

I should have allowed my gut to doubt you.

And now I have to relearn how to live without you.

To only come out to friends that aren't my friends.

Suggesting that I lie cheat and pretend.

Followed by wolves who look like men.

They always find me.

I don't know why I always have to be the kind me.

I always try to love kindly but it's hard not becoming everything you hate
when you don't even think to mind me.

You remind me of overwhelming assignments.

You remind me of motorcycle consignments.

You remind me of frequent doctor appointments;

you are a disappointment.

I wish I could rid you with ointment.

I thank God for loving me through this disappointment.

I thank God that my mother was there for me.

My sisters held on and cared for me.

I thank God my father was absent during this moment in history.

I thank God for pug puppies and pug kisses.

I thank God that genies don't grant wishes,

because I would want everything that was wrong.

Every choice never seems to belong to me.

Other People's Problems

You said that you belonged to me.

You said you'd love me heavily,

and now this shipwreck is everything but heavenly.

I could multiply all of your good by seventy,

and it would still never mean shyt.

You were my worst investment deposit.

Now please leave my closet.

Words-4-tha-Wise- Dealing With The Premeditation Of A Break Up:

1. Do not assume that people will change simply because you want them to

2. Taking some time to be single is a good idea if you feel that you need space

3. Listen to advice but make your own choices

4. Worry about how you feel even if it hurts someone else's feelings

5. Listen to your intuition

6. Do not sacrifice your peace for anyone

7. Frequent visits to your insecurities will make your relationship inconvenient

8. Realize that it may be you that is not ready to handle the weight of a relationship (Not knowing how to trust)

9. Do not lower your standards

10. Being alone might be scary, but heavy internal conflict will steal your joy

Break Off

Today I take a break,

don't care if I'm late,

my mind must retake its serenity.

I need just me times infinity.

I'm taking time off from being aloof off in my own intentions.

Today there shall be no interventions.

Today the integrity of your smile will go unmentioned by me,

and I suggest you not try me.

I'm finding that I'm over dependant on every remnant of how others may feel about whatever may be real to them.

Not going to squint my eyes in order to see man;

we are monsters applauding at our own concerts,

trying to introvert my natural extrovert.

I don't even care to share my dessert in despair,

won't even attempt to tear myself away from my mood and my own thoughts,

so for now I will step back into my box,

turn all of my fluffy pleasantries into rocks,

because I have now reached the over,

I don't wish to associate sad with sober,

no longer wish to retain possession of the controller,

I aspire to be muted.

While my mind ruffles through the disputed,

and deprogram what has been computed into me.

Don't feel that I care if you're into me,

Other People's Problems

my silence will lead to another win for me.

My life will play out accordingly.

My love will be the unicorn you often dream about.

My touch will be the withdraw you often feign about,

and conversation will be the silence that you wish to talk about.

I no longer wish to talk about my life the way that I choose,

with the help of God and if any should choose to slip away,

They will go knowing that they could never say that Ashley ever loved anyone less than she was supposed to,

or that she's selfish stuck up,

or ever turned her nose to depression or deceit,

because ill ways are not my virtue.

My popping personality now has a curfew,

and free samples have been removed from the menu,

but don't worry about me,

please, continue.

Words-4-tha-Wise- How To Recognize When It Is Time To Be Alone:

1. When you are easily irritated and do not understand why

2. When you start to become drawn into other people's drama

3. Overeating

4. When you begin to criticize yourself

5. You are tired all of the time

6. When you are constantly finding someone to be around every moment of every day

7. When you have been busy all day

8. When people you trust notice a change in you

9. When you are quick tempered

10. When it becomes difficult to complete simple things

Used To

I remember when I used to be proud of myself,

but now I clap silently in the dark in, what is supposed to be, my prime.

Yet all the time I'm haunted by my choices.

Voices from better days seem to have the nastiest way of expressing that you are no longer doing well.

So don't say that when people ask.

Yes you are blessed and yes this test is difficult to pass.

But life is lived through dim lighting when you mix sad emotions with bad timing.

I guess I'm too confused to know what this really means.

I guess I'm so unfocused on every single dream,

that I'm starting to tear at my own seams.

Pulling at the dreaded thread in hopes that I do not become unraveled, listening to the sounds of the night whilst I peel out over gravel.

Broken glasses and peek a boo asses that traipse out of midnight taverns. This life or particular pattern is aloof in my mind while I stomach the courage to find my right mind,

and the right time at the same time.

I can no longer drink wine simply because it is available.

I cannot simply rewind the time I'm surely incapable.

But I'm not ok with this present.

Yet it is my gift, it's my present,

but I am not present enough to speak up and be counted,

for I have lost the way to what I thought was my happiness.

But like the mouse and her misplaced cheese,

I must not linger near my disease,

but the taste of rot has overcome my thoughts,

and I no longer know what smogless day looks like.

I simply feel like saying no.

I simply feel like letting go of all my promises,

breaking ties with all of my mental processes,

and sitting still in the company of me.

No longer will anything come before me I hope.

No longer do I appreciate drowning in debris simply because I do not have the courage to decline the dip.

While my friends and family sip tea to my situation.

Cheers to infatuation for being my greatest downfall.

Good night to the theatrics for you will be my favorite last call.

But this won't be my end all.

I just pray I never pre-fall and like it.

And when my tears start to run races down my face I'll be sure to wipe it away.

I so long for the day when I used to believe in my actions.

But instead of remembering my reactions,

I reinstate fractions of who I use to be.

I can no longer act as though the future does not look like rubble to me. Why are my thoughts starting to crumble to me?

I hate when I mumble to me.

My thoughts choose to rumble with me.

When will I find the strength to get tired.

Why do I still see purpose in the job when I fired myself.

I guess I unknowingly check out of myself.

Other People's Problems

If I can't take care of myself,

then to the world, I will never be of any help.

Words-4-tha-Wise- Acknowledging When It Is Time To Grow Up:

1. When you regularly ask your parents for money

2. You don't know how to budget your money

3. When you don't have a job that can cover your own monthly expenses

4. Do you spend most of your time playing games

5. If you sleep until noon without a valid reason

6. When you are always complaining

7. If you still do not know how to cook and properly feed yourself

8. Always feeling entitled to everything

9. Never take responsibility for yourself

10. Being unreliable

Young Girl Hope

Little girls with attitudes learn later in life that it's not always a fight that is needed.

Neglect from the right one can make a spiteful one conceited.

Too puffed up on looks to ever truly feel affection.

Too faded to ever truly see one's own reflection.

We're in need of protection.

Constantly searching for perfect.

Giving up too soon because we don't even feel worth it.

Worth the energy it takes to actually find and love yourself,

because soon self love turns into feminism,

which is a special kind of hell.

Then next comes lesbianism,

but I'm not the type to have sex with females as well,

but how do you explain a feminist who still gets boy crazy?

How easy it is to decipher subliminal remarks from a mark who has been predisposed to self neglect?

Love him more than you love yourself,

so that he'll never forget that he needs you.

Somehow I feel that is something I need to do.

Not enough sense to take my own advice but I have some for you.

Barely treating my bank account right but I have a few dollars for you.

It's funny how females always seem to keep a stack,

of friends around who talk about us behind our back,

and we somehow equate that,

with being real.

Other People's Problems

Does it truly feel good to act ugly?

How can a bitch be fine and lovely,

when she doesn't even love what she looks like?

Looks like our investments are only temporary feel goods.

Getting just enough pleasure to feel good.

Making just enough money to look good.

but refuse to eat right in order to live good.

Refuse to think twice because right now feels good.

The future has always been so taxing to think about.

I think I want a house,

while back at my momma´s house.

Fearing that dreams will be the future my dreams dream about.

I like to let love feel me out.

Let love tell you about all of the times I've always been open.

Every time my real feelings were left unspoken was because I needed to be just still enough for my love pouch to reopen.

Finding solace in destruction while I'm constantly re-coping.

Revolting against societal norms that deem me as smart.

From the day I was born,

I was perfect in form,

then my poor little mind became addicted to porn.

Became addicted to lust.

Pawned a coin named trust,

so that I could afford us;

So us could exist.

Even if just through a kiss.

Other People's Problems

My heart will love you always,

But now my call you somehow missed.

The love you claimed we had seemed to fade in the mist.

But every single time I was down for the risk.

Entering situations that I'm "strong enough to handle."

Complicating my life for a blunt and a sample.

When you need a hand to hold I'm so sorry because my hands are full.

With being a handful in his life.

So with the rest of the change in my pocket,

I shall show loyalty by making sure my man is full,

and when that man is done,

another episode now done.

A laundry list of what to do next time and my broken self is what I've won.

New horizons eclipsed by the sun.

A broken spirit for years to come.

Only to settle for independent loneliness,

or for love that will never feel done,

never feel real,

because I have allowed the devil to manipulate how I feel.

that's why my ass is so soft,

because my head is too hard.

Looking to repair a broken woman you don't have to look far.

Just count the pieces of trash she has in the body of her car.

Keep track of every trinket she always forgets to discard.

She's just trying to find all of her broken pieces even when she overlooks her heart.

Words-4-tha-Wise- How To Not Allow Obstacles To Deter Your Decision Making:

1. You should be able to identify what the issues are

2. You should know everyone who is involved

3. Be able to recognize what it is that you have to lose

4. Understand what your options are

5. Determine which option will result in a better or positive result

6. Develop a consistent moral mentality that strives toward what is right

7. Be able to execute the right thing to do

8. Do not rationalize any situation in order to become comfortable

9. Be aware of the impact your actions may have on others

10. Do unto others as you would have them do unto you

Caught Up In The Middle

I have developed a fear for my life.

Nothing ever seems to feel right.

Who I am could never be right.

Each love in human form masking land mines to ensure that storm comes
for the ashes,

after Ash is half past crazy,

or must have lost her mind.

I'm starting to lose faith in being kind.

I'm starting to turn into the kind of woman you find on the other side how.
You're way too good to live this bad.

My convictions and indecisions are what make me mad.

Re-living uncomfortable moments in my life make me sad.

I've never trusted a man because I've never trusted dad.

I have never appropriately dealt with any of my pain.

I relive the same traumas but I swear they're not the same,

but I swear I'm to blame for all of them.

My impulse and flesh I follow them.

My pride and guilt I swallow them.

It's hard trying to be a part when you're not of them.

I wish I truly knew the rewards from better decision making.

Maybe I wouldn't be carrying debt while my hearts slowly breaking.

My job slowly robbing me of the life I can't afford to live yet.

Frustration laced in every unfinished project.

Now becoming an object of ridicule and popularity,

that means everybody stares at me.

Other People's Problems

You love me to death or you don't care for me.

Truly amazed to find out who is truly there for me.

Bad vibes bring a need for therapy.

Ever been seriously told that you need therapy.

I need a heart that won't break,

that's therapy.

I need loved ones he won't take,

that scares me.

I need his love so that my soul he can take,

that seems fair to me.

Just pray my current situations turn into memories or fabrications of what people might think they may know.

I'm learning not to ask for answers that I don't want to know.

I pray I make every right turn when my spirit says go,

but for now I'll just take an apartment that comes with a stove.

I feel that I may be getting restless with no place to go.

<u>Words-4-tha-Wise- When You Don't Believe Your "Someday" Is Coming:</u>

1. Ask yourself what it is that you would love to be

2. Decide that you are going to commit

3. Believe that you are capable of achieving the end result

4. Change your negative outlook on things into positive ones

5. Practice the art of saying no

6. Figure out your to-do list that leads to your end result

7. Give yourself enough time to feel your feelings and organize your thoughts

8. Place your desires and needs first

9. Look at the success of others as a reminder to keep on achieving

10. A mistake is just a misguided step that needs to be redirected

Perfect World

I want to live in a world where I'll always have money to eat.

Where the love of my life doesn't feel tempted enough to cheat.

Where I can trust every single individual that I ever meet,

and where one always has time to visit family every week.

A world where perfect daughters treat their mothers like queens,

and where every child knows too well what fatherhood means;

and not through fatherhood memes.

I would love to wake up everyday handcuffed to my dreams.

Become addicted to meditation, or perhaps play on a softball team.

In a world that measures wealth in smiles.

Where every hard time has an instructional file,

on how to live life and not hurt for a while.

Where every child may have a place to play,

and every parent a beautiful home to stay.

Every house with everything in its place.

Where friendship is honored like a mother's China case.

Where every time and place has a moment for clarity.

Where every friend has gum they can share with me.

Where living as an adult doesn't have to put a scare in me.

Where love is abundant and we lack the knowledge of scarcity.

I would love to be a woman who received respect from every man.

Where a diet and healthy spending is not something I have to plan.

I pray that when there's an argument it be can solved through shaking hands.

Where pointing fingers is a sign of peace.

Other People's Problems

Where my scalp doesn't have to be greased.

Where cars and property don't have to be leased,

and all innocent citizens granted their release.

A land with no cold weather and warm sunny skies.

Where the vulnerability of a soul doesn't leak through the eyes.

Where evil can never find the perfect disguise.

Where every worker never stresses the time and whether it flies.

where we believe in honesty instead of anticipating lies.

Where we can choose to let go and walk away from harmful ties,

without batting an eye.

Without having to try so hard at being the perfect person.

Where perfect people talk in person.

May every unwed remain a virgin,

and where self love is never questioned and always for certain.

Words-4-tha-Wise- How To Live In Peace:

1. Understand that peace is living without violence, while embracing respect and tolerance

2. Stop seeking to impose power or insert your opinion/agenda on someone else

3. Trying to control others leads to conflict

4. Make a list of fun activities to explore

5. The only way to power is through peace

6. Compliment someone everyday

7. Learn how to negotiate

8. Learn conflict resolution

9. Learn how to communicate assertively

10. Understand that the people around you are capable of living a great life without your help

Let it Go

To all the phones placed upside down on your side of the bed,

to every single side piece that borrows love from others´ beds,

to all the negative self talk that I allow to stew in my head,

I'm going to write you down and throw you away,

because that's what my abundance blog said.

Words-4-tha-Wise-How To Let Go Of Anything:

1. Understand that in order to move on you must make room

2. Try to understand the true value of something that may/may not bring value into your life

3. Be honest with yourself about what is truly worth keeping

4. Do not feel obligated to receive every gift that is presented to you

5. Figure out how to operate in your current setting

6. Don't feel obligated to hold onto things that you don't absolutely love

7. Understand to only keep what you truly need

8. Don't feel guilty denying external baggage

9. Do not create space for items with potential use for an eventually that may never come

10. A clear space will grant a clear mind

Not Having It

The cards are not in my favor.

This relationship is not the flavor I wish to savor any longer.

I should not have stayed a minute longer.

Unfortunately your will is a tad bit stronger.

Your nerve is little bit longer than my ability to walk away.

I have a complaint to compensate for everyday,

and it never seems as though I get my way.

I lose my days waiting for you.

Willing to forgo dating for you.

I guess I'll just get back to mating with you.

Conversations with you,

contemplating with you all the things we go through,

because men tend to always do what they gone do.

But women, guess what, we love you any way.

Women our hearts stay where we're not meant to stay.

Women our souls participate in games we're not meant to play.

We're not meant to love, break, and cry this way.

You will forever ask the question why this way.

Why this day does my heart openly bleed without scabbing?

Why when I walk away do you start grabbing?

Why when I go out do you start tabbing?

Wondering if whether or not someone is out here jabbin;

anticipating stabbing.

I'm just out here finally finding out where my worth is at.

143

Other People's Problems

Slowly trying not to give myself a heart attack.

tired of moving forward and looking back.

Tired of seeing the same love still where it's at.

Tired of wanting companionship and not having that.

I'm not having that!

Words-4-tha-Wise- How To Move On From Repetitive Problems:

1. Tell yourself "no" when you start to experience negative thoughts

2. Know that self-doubt is there to keep you from changing

3. Share meals with people who make you feel good

4. Leaving your thoughts internal will not grant you the room to organize them

5. Write things down in a journal to keep things clear and realistic

6. People do not realistically care too much about your personal choices and decisions, because they have their own life

7. Find an atmosphere that is enthusiastic, motivating, and optimistic

8. Setbacks are only temporary

9. Study material on subjects you do not feel confident about

10. Remember to correct your steps along the way

Depression Anonymous

Hi my name is Ashley and I am depressed.

I've been super stressed,

my heart's a mess,

and I barely get dressed for my days anymore.

I'm pretty sure my cure resides in the mouth of a breathing miracle.

If only I had wings to fly there.

If only I knew it was ok to cry there,

so that I won't die there,

waiting for me to catch up.

Everyday I swear I try to wake up with the best of intentions,

but life becomes hard to mention when every story is uncomfortable to talk about.

Every problem is something I don't want anyone to know about.

So it becomes hard when I look up for someone to help me out.

I'd rather hug a drought then lead anyone to believe that I was ever helpless.

It just helps less when you lose the stamina you had for your dreams.

When you hit the brink of destroying teams,

when you hit the floor and don't know what it means to get back up again because you need to.

Hard work won't pay off until you do,

and yes that means every cent you owe.

Everyday I grow by constant force and life lessons.

When I read the blogs this was not what I was expecting.

I am protecting what's left of my common sense,

Other People's Problems

while slipping into present tense.

While purchasing promises that were meant to hold you and love you on all days.

I've watched bad vibes disturb all days of this haze that I freakin stew in.

Thank god I kept pursuing something.

Thank god I still believe in something.

I'm just afraid I won't be able to have that one thing.

because that one thing might turn into nothing,

and nothing in life is what I choose.

I pray I'm not addicted to being misused.

It even makes it worse sometimes trying to be happy on cue.

Especially after missing a payment after it's due.

Wondering whether or not to get a new dude.

Figuring out how to change my attitude.

When talking to customer service I won't try to be so rude.

Moving home with my momma will not change my altitude.

I promise I'll try to stop believing in lies so that I won't be so damn confused.

Just waiting on me to come back right now.

No need to rehash or recap right now.

I need to get a hold of my life somehow.

Words-4-tha-Wise- How To Help Yourself Out Of A Funk:

1. Write down your goals

2. Get adequate sleep

3. Perform an hour of cardio whenever possible; if possible

4. Stop holding onto resentment, anger, or regret

5. Make a list of all of things in your life that you are grateful for

6. Receive at least 30 minutes of sunlight everyday

7. Drink 2-3 Liters of water a day (four 19.9 oz water bottles)

8. Take time to love, appreciate, and listen to your friends; this creates a healthy support system

9. Read everyday

10. Write everyday

Your Type

I always seem to be somebody's one who got away.

Apparently my first impressions say "good catch."

Explains to his soul that I'm a keeper.

Hoping your spirit will never sleep on me.

I guess that's why he gets nervous if he doesn't own my every night.

I guess somehow he knew how to survive every fight.

I'm also aware that my statistics precede me.

My personality somehow makes you need me.

I would succumb to most requests so that you would have all that you needed.

You hate the fact that I'm conceited,

and that without me you feel defeated.

Always here to do my best to make sure you were always treated.

You've always needed someone like me,

so it must be me.

Who else gone love your soul like me?

Who else can conquer more of your heart than me?

Even if I left your ass for years your dreams will still see me.

You'll want to know the quest to my every secret.

Follow me around,

And as for my stuff I'm sure you'll keep it.

So excited about having me that I've met all the family,

and we get along happily.

you're heart prays my heart never packs and leaves,

and branches and leaves on your tree have fallen bitter or brittle to me.

Other People's Problems

Can hardly fathom why you're stuck on me but would gladly trade you places just to see how good I might be.

Of marriage and children is what you always speak.

With me by your side is how you want to spend every night of every week. Every kiss upon my cheek is yours by reservation.

You're goal will be to knock all opponents out of consideration.

To have me to yourself is your destination,

and my face to your chest is your medication.

My princess ways will draw your adoration,

And my jealous heart will scream for validation.

Our love is education.

I learn every day in our world,

and you'll always seek to be my end all.

You'll open your heart so that I will have somewhere I can fall.

You'll try to discreetly ignore my incoming call.

Praying that it was just a friend that just called.

You'll pray that I never fall for anyone ever.

You'll lie if it means we'll always be together.

I'll haunt your thoughts and have you screaming never.

Never will you find another angel again.

Never will you have another female best friend.

Never will I ever ignore you if I ever saw you again,

and if or when it ends,

you'll find loopholes to be my friend,

and ask me sweetly to extend,

the deadline so that our love can mend.

Other People's Problems

You will cherish the way that I can grace all of your years.

A God gifted companion to help fight all your fears.

With enough strength to endure everyone of our tears,

so that decades from now we can clink and say cheers;

and that's if we don't become destroyed by our peers.

Words-4-tha-Wise - How To Be Selective:

1. Stop fearing the outcome of any option

2. It is better to rely on instinct when making a decision

3. Consider how your options make you feel

4. Do research on a few other alternative options

5. Make sure that you don't stray too far from the goal that you are deciding for

6. Do not hold onto things/options just because you have spent a lot of time on them, feel free to change

7. Construct "What if?" scenarios

8. Don't let others have the final say on what is best for you

9. It is always better to minimize options (process of elimination)

10. Do not shy away from getting a professional opinion

Remember Your Power

The next time you forget who you are,

while sitting outside of your job in your car,

on your way home,

remember that you are not alone.

You are vibration dressed in intuition.

your vision gives birth to new law.

You are highly sought,

often caught,

and never kept.

you are single because you take the weight of your own opinion seriously.

We come together when we want our life to collaborate with legacy;

with heavily anticipated perfection,

matched with participation.

The only way out is the way through,

and the only way in goes through you.

So tell your company to take their shoes off at the door.

We no longer need to study every man that's in this world.

Take your world and go find you.

do whatever it is that your heart would love to do.

she will thank you with long overdue energy.

She will bless your mornings with clarity and every month with progression,

every year with better than before and the rest of your life with better decisions.

Your peace of mind can be found when you carry wisdom.

Wisdom illustrates the story of you.

153

Other People's Problems

how to overcome your pain when you don't know what to do.

Always count your time in threes,

some for them but more for me,

and one for He.

By he, I mean God.

The creator of every consequence as well as speech.

Karma will do her best to harm you while outside of His reach.

Substance is how you spell hello.

Your goals are where you're trying to go,

and ambition will help you get there.

Self doubt will help you sit there.

Your demons will convince you that you don't care about the future,

and a greedy heart will always be plucked before it has matured.

It's hard to pick up the pieces in order to restore.

Your heart shall endure what you take it through.

If you can't see the flags regret will break it through.

so accept,

breathe,

and move up in order to make it through.

Words-4-tha-Wise- How To Embrace A Paradigm Shift:

1.   Take some time to relax and take in the new environment

2. Take ample time to take special care of yourself

3. Create a plan and remember to stick to it

4. Be open to learning new things

5. Try something that you would not normally try/do

6. Do not adopt everyone else's advice on what you should be doing with your life

7. Learn to be comfortable with uncertainty

8. Decisions that you are going to make will not gaurantee a positive or negative outcome

9. Be willing to let go clutter, clothes, and etc

10. Let go of things that keep you anchored to your past

Sew A Seed

I want to wake up to paid bills and financial freedom.

I seek to live free,

be free,

and build my Queendom.

I plan to plant smiles and understanding on every platform I receive.

Follow step after step so that I can always achieve.

I wish to see growth in the mind of every spirit I meet.

Receive long kisses on my forehead and cheek.

My plan is to be happy,

my goal is stay that way.

I'll make the best decisions,

so that my future will have a place to stay.

A place to breathe and become one with the sun.

Think of all my enemies before deleting everyone.

Make sure I tell my heart and mind to come.

Make sure that they can get along better so that I can get my shyt together.

I need to know that home is right where I left it,

and if I gave you my heart and you kept it,

just make sure that you always take care.

I will be sent mind and energy compliments,

and all of it will be compliments of my gratitude.

I apologize if my attitude ever got in the way,

but today's a new day and that day is Tuesday.

From that day on everyday will be fresh,

Other People's Problems

and when I come home to my head,

I won't see a mess.

I pray to always feel bangin in a body con dress,

and that there will always be a mic for me to come and express.

I will have ceilings that have attics that scratch the surface of heaven.

On this journey called life I was given the number seven.

So I guess that means I'm on my way to almost there,

and while riding on ascension I get to keep the fact that I care.

With 4 solid souls that promise to always be there.

Waking up to affirmations,

that breathe the word positive.

Always standing up on my truth that makes me not only sure but positive.

I pray to give every word that I know a place to sit,

and every spirit who wants to grow a place to stay,

and I pray that it will always stay that way!

<u>Words-4-tha-Wise- How To Breathe Life Into Yourself:</u>

1. Be very specific about what you would like in your life

2. Only speak positively

3. Understand that the best encouragement comes from within

4. Tell yourself that you are blessed and amazing

5. Compliment yourself on the way you look

6. Plan trips or occasions that you will enjoy by yourself

7. Look into reading motivational/inspirational books and/or materials

8. Listen to your gut feelings

9. Always look for the bigger picture

10. Spend time in nature (if applicable)

Snooze Button

You ever hang around conscious people and ever feel like you're not black enough?

Not that you're not black enough,

but your black doesn't go to bat for black liberties.

Your black doesn't fight civil disparities.

You're black apparently is the reason why white folks need clarity,

because not all black people are bad since they've met you.

Your hair tends to slick back just right so not you.

It wasn't you I was talking to when I called you a nappy headed hoe,

and if your complexion is 2 shades too dark you gotta go.

But if you smile sweetly the kind white people will let you go.

I guess I was the niece my Uncle Tom never spoke about.

When you're the only blacky in sight that is all others seem to talk about.

I guess I should die for not falling in love with dr sebi.

I simply went natural because the damage of a perm was too heavy.

so now I should be an activist for natural hair.

I guess I'm the reason white people feel it's ok to stare.

I guess I'm the reason they feel so comfortable touching our hair.

I'm sorry my role model wasn't Angela Davis,

and I know black people shouldn't even say this,

but I love being black whether it is popular or not.

I hate when black people say that hate and anger are taught,

but refuse to love each other.

Go to rally's to support the fight for their brother,

but don't even visit their mothers' once a month.

Other People's Problems

You scream "Black Power" as if now for once,

black women can feel proud to call you our black man.

As if for once we can go off and make black plans,

create a black clan,

that grows to love all creatures and occasions.

Why should I fight for black love that would rather be black and Asian?

Why should I fight for black men when they still fuck Caucasians?

Oh I guess since you own a dashiki that you are now the black persuasion,

and on our first date I should let you induct me into the nation.

Because apparently you know all that there is to know.

You've read all the right books that will show,

that the only way to be black is to be in the know.

The only way to be black is to disown every comfort you've ever known.

That the only way to be black is to suffer along the ride.

The only way to be black would be to rebuke Jesus because apparently white people lied.

They have all the money,

so now our funds we feel we should hide.

we become black and red while our transgressions collide,

while our spirits align, with a deeper purpose.

I don't believe in practicing hate but I know I'm far from perfect,

but which avenue towards black supremacy makes the battle seem worth it?

What about us women who pray to one day have a family?

Or our current generation searching for financial freedom,

who is really living happily?

Other People's Problems

We scantily slide by on hopes of feeling relevant,

while guarding our closet life because we seek our own prevalence.

I don't really care which path is perfect.

Will never really know if anything I say will be worth the confusion.

Just don't promise me an illusion,

that comes with honesty when we fear of the white man's intrusion.

Be faithful while holding hands with the women you devote your fusion,

and tell us how home will never be home until love is our only conclusion.

Words-4-tha-Wise- How To Increase Love Amongst Black People:

1. Start by ALWAYS having something nice to say to each other

2. Carry the belief that you love all Black people

3. Accept that not all people, even some black people, are going to like black people

4. Surround yourself with beautiful images of black people

5. Become a part of a positive black community

6. Create a positive black community

7. Look at the tone of your skin as a fingerprint rather than a status symbol

8. Do not TRY to become a stereotypical type of black person with required tastes and emotions that are not natural to who you truly are

9. The more we show love to each other, the higher the vibration of our people will be

10. Be prepared to set aside differences that you may have amongst other Black people, and be willing to contribute to the strength of a loving, compassionate, and forgiving Black Community. (Key to Black Survival)

Trade Your Heart

What if he realizes his worth before I do?

What if he believed a good friend was my side dude?

What if I was always nonchalantly rude all the time?

What if I never called, none of the time?

What if I never claimed you or called you mine?

Would you still mind when I ask you for head?

Would he still sleep in the same bed with me?

Would he spend time arguing just to argue about spending more time with me.

Would you be mad if a threesome with two men was fine with me?

Would you still feel fine with me.

Would you stifle your tears just to share laughs with me?

Would you mind if I never kept cash with me?

Would you carry me?

Can I come to where you stay?

Bring all my stuff then leave all day.

Would you feel hopeless trying to figure out why you still love me this way?

Will you call me out,

when I manipulate your mouth to say sorry for something I did?

Would you mind if I already had two kids,

and shared a few cribs with some ex men,

and still sometimes text them,

and every now and then sex them.

Would you mind if I lied about not wanting them?

as if him wanting me was completely one sided,

163

Other People's Problems

even tho it was my legs I once let him divide.

Would you kindly fill my tank,

Give me money from your bank,

Even when I never thank you for anything.

What if I lied to you about actually wanting a wedding ring?

Be unrealistic and tell you that you're my everything.

Then not call or tell you anything,

when I just don't feel like coming home;

because after all I'm also grown.

What if I never showed concern for the fact that you always feel alone?

What if I barely answered my phone?

What if I didn't watch my tone when talking to you in front of your friends?

Or stressed you to the point where the only sane thing to do is end us.

while I beg and plead for you to mend us,

and shared no responsibility for your lack of trust.

Would you still love me the way that you do?

Do you think it would ever be possible to love me the way I love you?

Words-4-tha-Wise- How To Empathize With The Opposite Sex:

1. Understand that characteristics of both sexes are summed up by percentages and do not apply to every single male or female

2. The way we naturally are and the way were raised as children will play a part in how to determine our sensitivity levels; not the fact that we are male or female

3. It is important for all sexes to have emotional relief

4. It is important for all sexes to build emotional and spiritual strength

5. We should all strive to know ourselves better before becoming emotionally involved in anyone's life

6. Everyone deserves personal space/boundaries

7. Spend platonic time with members of the opposite sex in order to understand them better as individuals

8. Know that trust, loyalty, and security must be earned and built overtime

9. If you treat all men/women as though they are the same, it is because you are still the same

10. There is not one human being in the world that can give you everything that you want, and there will be moments in life when it is necessary to be alone

Black Ass

You're so pretty for a dark skin,

but you black as fuck,

and I don't really give a fuck,

but I've never dated a chocolate like you before.

I usually go for light skin, light eyes, and cute whores,

but a queen is what I see when I look at you.

You're so beautiful that I want 10 kids with you,

and when I'm ready I think one day I wanna marry you,

but still I can't quite figure out why my mother seems to like you.

See I was raised around light skins who don't tend to fuck with people who are shaded just like you,

but you,

You're so beautiful that you're different.

So I guess that makes you different.

So I guess you're qualified to be one of my women.

You're skin is pretty so I guess you got the right type of melanin,

but my head is in the heart of this generation.

I see team darkskin has peaked through segregation.

I see that your skin is so evenly saturated.

I see that those draws might be easily penetrated,

so I'll make sure that you know that I'm not here just for sexing you.

I promise I lied in whatever text I was texting you.

But you know that you the realist and that's why I mess with you,

I hate my own skin but I seem to mess with you.

I don't see less in you,

but that light skin in that dress got me thinking about stressing you.

Got me thinking bout depressing you.

Going farther than just being cheated.

Your queendom and resource is what I've always needed.

I apologize that my desire for something different makes you feel defeated.

I'm sorry that I was never the lover you always needed,

And that my hate for myself makes you feel mistreated.

But don't you ever get too cocky, too confident, or conceited,

Because you're still a mud duck,

a black bitch;

So receive it.

Words-4-tha-Wise- How To Fall In Love With Your Dark Black Skin (Any Skin Tone):

1. Stop comparing the shade of your skin to others

2. There is an infinite amount of beauty in this world that cannot be defined by one definition or one person

3. Surround yourself with positive and beautiful images that look like you

4. Do not be concerned with anyone's opinion of you outside of your own

5. Repeat affirmations of beauty to yourself daily

6. Colorism is a social disease and not your personal problem

7. Avoid stereotyping any shade of skin

8. Tell yourself that you accept and love yourself everyday

9. Understand that most people are insecure about who they are regardless of skin color

10. If you maintain internal beauty you will always have external beauty

Girls To Women

You see I'm starting to learn that,

a romantic suicidal is born when a young girl starts foregoing bibles,

and starts creating rivals with girlfriends in common.

Premeditated neglect is the seed that grows a lack of self respect.

That leads to promiscuity and self neglect.

Always arriving too late to self reflect.

We begin to mix our value with vixen.

While broken hearts avoid proper fixing.

Where you wish you had the time to listen to what momma used to say.

Maybe I should have never skipped school that day.

Maybe I should have worked harder to stay where the piece of my mind,
pro creates an inner peace of mind,

that would have lead me to less confusion.

That was followed by the fast life exclusion,

that I should have never been a part of.

But man how fun that time was.

See my mind can't comprehend the way yours does.

I would always fuck up because I always wanted my father's attention.

I wanted to be my mother's favorite mention.

But now I succeed in chaos.

My life needs a new boss.

My love for self can no longer be lost.

Too damn concerned with lip gloss.

I need another coin toss.

That ends in me using my head instead of my tail.

Other People's Problems

So that my life can progress and prevail past describing sex in detail.

Sometimes I swear it sucks being female.

It's funny how any man at any age,

feels comfortable talking to women in any way.

Forcing us all to accept their brutish ways.

Then walk away with a wink like it will be ok.

That shyt is not ok.

Harassment is spelled that way.

Young girls forego trust that way.

Young girls learn lust that way.

Before we learn how to even pray.

So if you see a pretty girl,

let her stay that way.

When we're not treated like we're people we turn into bitches that way.

Think of all the young women who walk the streets alone.

Frantically looking, searching through her phone,

praying that she'll make it all the way home.

Coming face to face with boys who don't like no's.

Convincing us one by one that it's ok to be hoes.

Turning beauties into hoes.

Somehow we find comfort in vulgar clothes.

We find fake refuge in the stories we pray you'll never know.

Finding ease in fornication praying the first heartbreak never shows.

That one cousin that use to touch her, she prays you'll never know.

Now when met with correction her heart says no.

Other People's Problems

Now when her shirts and skirts are too tight her mouth says so.

Now every opportunity for love her mind says go.

Avoiding reality is how her life says cope.

Her lungs are most certainly filled with dope.

Loss of love equals loss of self,

equals loss of hope.

She laughs at her future because she feels her life's a joke.

As a teen when I received many disappointments from a man.

I believe that unknowingly I created a spiteful plan.

To break the minds and hearts of every single man.

Then awake to every morning to wash the blood from my hands.

Barely loving ourselves at all but believing that with you we can.

My heart hurts for young women who aren't protected in this world.

We grow up to be the woman you see while harboring a broken little girls.

so men, in our company have a lil more respect,

and women don't talk down on another women while talking to the opposite sex,

and parents make sure that's it's your children you spend time and protect,

because loving through neglect or disrespect,

will guarantee that your child will be next.

Words-4-tha-Wise-How To Protect Our Young Children From Sexual Abuse:

1. Encourage children to talk about their day

2. Build an exchange of trust by talking to your children everyday

3. Sexual offenders tend to come off as charming and friendly towards children in order to gain parental trust

4. Sexual predators tend to be close to, if not inside, the home

5. Get to know your child's friends and their parents

6. If possible have more than one chaperone or babysitter

7. All adults should confront suspicious behavior between a minor and an adult

8. Teach your children that danger may come from anyone

9. Teach children what acceptable interactions and boundaries look like (even when interacting with other older children)

10. Refusing to sleep, eat, interact with others, acting out regularly, or excessive peeing in the bed may be signs of sexual abuse

Weak Sauce

For the record,

I left you because you were weak.

I don't like the fact that you felt you had to cheat.

I appreciate the fact that you always tried to be sweet,

but it was the gap between your feet that lead us to distraction.

It was your head so wrapped in dysfunction that you forgot we were supposed to be royalty.

You asked me to live this life with you so I promised you my loyalty.

You tried to uncoil me,

rather than understand that I am a woman that tends to emasculate almost every man I've ran into.

I guess you weren't to sure of who the flowers were supposed to be sent to.

I left you because you had it not.

Our obligation you forgot to hold onto,

and now I must move on to prepare myself to be a Queen.

I wanted you to come along and be my King,

so I could love you and give you everything,

but that was always impossible.

Your kisses I still often think about.

Our distorted forever I can't help but dream about.

I'm just confused on why you couldn't help me out of my controlling nature. Apparently we forgot how to treat each other.

Maybe I didn't respect your mother for loving me more than you did.

Now I feel all alone and look stupid,

because I said no to cheating because I thought u did.

173

Other People's Problems

Why can't there be some sort of understanding?

Why didn't I understand that you weren't my man in God's planning?

How did I say yes while always demanding that you shouldn't even love me at all?

You were eloquent and cute and that made me fall.

Now I'm left to a wall of disappointed homegirls.

Now I'm finding "you'll always have me" girls.

Now I'm getting "I've always loved your beautiful life girl,"

but not from the right guy.

You were wrong for the job and I knew that,

but my addiction to love made me think we outgrew that,

and now I'm mad because you had to do that.

Knowing that I always knew that.

You would never hesitate to make me feel good when you felt like it.

Now I'm moving on like I should but I'm hurt by it.

Now my love is scared again,

because I know how bad I want to try it again.

I want to be loved by one great man.

I would love a man who always knew when it was time to take charge.

A busy man isn't always a man who works hard.

Sometimes he works her.

Don't mistake it for a miscommunication,

this man has been unfaithfully fornicating.

Or at least mines was.

So I guess that doesn't mean that yours does;

but he sure does spring up anger and confusion.

Other People's Problems

Forcing you to believe in illusions,

because he doesn't want you to come to the conclusion,

that he loves you, but your just his love infusion.

Your love fills him with energy to go run the streets.

Sure he's thinking of you while he has whores to meet.

Sure he's talking about you right before he goes to creep.

And sure he'll selfie with you and call you every minute of every week,

but right before he meets up with his other.

Will lie to you and tell you he's going to hang with his brother.

Will lie and say that he fell asleep at his mother's.

Will lie to you and say "that's your hair on this pillow cover."

Will lie to you until the day he becomes discovered.

The evidence he will try to hide from you.

Go out and fuck a bitch right after making love to you,

and you never really see what it does to you,

until it's too late.

Now we walking around harboring his mistakes.

Now we mad at every time he came in late.

Now we mad because we said hell no to other dates,

and now you starve because you gave what was left on your plate.

I hate a man who covers his lies with gifts.

Can't stand a boy who pulls over time shifts,

but never has change to spare but can always go and wash his whip.

Somehow has the gas to make it through every trip.

I honestly believe these men see a woman in you.

Other People's Problems

They lie to themselves about how manly they think they are and will speak badly to you.

Never support anything that you do.

Never have the time to come through.

Never taking enough time to know you.

Trying to trap the Queen you are,

because queens like us hide out with scars,

meet men in bars,

take them in with or without cars,

and look to the stars for love in desperation.

Praying that this love will be the example for our generation.

Praying that God will allow this one last disobedient flirtation,

but ladies it's only because your marks are set too low.

We don't know how to love a man,

so we settle for boys.

Buying them food and stepping on their toys,

as we pick up after them and deal with they disrespectful ass boys.

I'm so tired of this misunderstanding.

I want a man who's concerned with understanding me.

Why is it that they expect us to stay at home,

be alone,

and only talk to them on our phones.

They seek to keep us unaware of how much we really don't know.

They seek to shield our eyes from lies they fear we might know,

and we settle for their tries even when we really want to go.

How does a lady get over a man?

Other People's Problems

She gets with her girls and she writes down a plan.

You go out and be fabulous right down to the T.

Build yourself up to be a Queen and be all that you can be.

Surround yourself with loving women and watch how strong you will be.

Don't settle for shyt you don't like.

Open your eyes so that you can see,

that beauty exists outside the confines of love.

You can have a man but remember to rise above.

Remember to always love yourself first.

Anything less will make your situation worse.

Don't worry if you feel you've lost all hope.

If you're a Queen and you know it, your life will be dope.

Just find a way to cope in the meanwhile.

Don't settle for confusion or denial.

Your are a gentile and shall be protected,

and our beloved Father whom you once neglected,

won't cease until your life is better.

So don't worry about your eyes becoming wetter.

You are a conqueror and can master any and all things.

That's why I left him;

he was too centered on small things.

That's why I left him.

Breathe slowly as the rhythm of your phone rings.

Be still and know to remain in the presence of tall queens.

Don't just pick out a man, wait for your mate.

Other People's Problems

Don't keep a man past his expiration date.

Take time for yourself it will never be too late,

and don't let him lie to you;

Your bitter girls are single because they once said yes to the same date.

Words-4-tha-Wise- How To Recognize Toxic People:

1. Very selfish in most or all situations

2. A desire or constant need to be right

3. They are constantly involved in problematic or dramatic situations playing the role of the victim

4. People who are comfortable with telling lies

5. People who are constantly convincing you that everything is your fault, or not their fault

6. People who are too eager to start a relationship

7. They do not take responsibility for their own shortcomings

8. They do not have nice things to say about others

9. People who cannot be straightforward

10. They do not have a natural respect for or they are not nice to others

Blessed With Understanding

I don't mind having problems.

I don't expect to be perfect,

but my standards are high because who I am is worth it.

Sometimes I fall short of being beautiful on the outside and within,

but I don't allow my struggle to defeat me,

it's only where my story begins.

I love everyone one I know whether they love me back or not,

but that's what you do when you're truly happy,

Or at least that's what I was taught.

I hate subliminal messages and detest being mad forever.

I suck at keeping in touch but in my mind we were always together.

I respect you all for where you stood and appreciate all the company.

If I'm not at my best right now its only because better is what was meant for me.

My drive can make me selfish,

and my confidence might project conceit,

but please don't mistake your insecurities with my willingness to succeed.

I commend you all for baring your burdens because life at times can be grim.

Just remember to take care of the scars on your welcome mat,

and be cautious of those you invite in.

<u>Words-4-tha-Wise- How To Be Selective With The Company You Keep:</u>

1. Spend time with people who can show you new and positive things

2. Spend time with those who share your values

3. Choose friends who have similar goals to yours

4. Befriend others who can help you become strong in areas where you are weak

5. Spend time with people who enjoy doing the same things you enjoy

6. Be close to those who are constantly seeking to grow

7. Keep people around who will be genuinely happy for you and your successes

8. Be friends with those who set goals and accomplish them

9. Know that you have a say in when to start friendship, but it is completely up to you to discontinue a friendship

10. Put into your friendships what you intend to get out of them

Complexities & Complications

You thought I could fix you but you were wrong again.

You made me believe it was ok to fall in love again.

Convincing me that in you, I would always have a friend.

Now my tears won't cease to fall because I can't pretend.

I can't attempt to believe that love for us was meant.

I gave you the benefit of the doubt so the rules I bent.

Heart broken by the pictures that were sent,

and now with God I repent.

I've called off so much I can barely pay my rent.

Now in our memories I have found a dent.

I need you to pick up your shyt from my apartment.

The love you lent,

without consent,

has messed with my head and now I can't stand a compliment.

Up against a wall I feel pent.

Right over my heart in your brand new car you went.

Not a single dollar was spent.

Now every text that you've sent,

means nothing so even the pictures I regret.

All of the times that I let,

you lie to my face I bet,

you felt like the victim but yet,

I can't help but feel that it was my trust you kept.

All the while knowing I could never forget,

Other People's Problems

how you always came back too late with that henny and bitch scent.

Our love was supposed to represent,

black love but now 1 cent is the value I see in you my friend.

Or should I say my newest ex boyfriend.

I was your toy that you bent.

I was your lie that you kept.

Under the rug your truth went.

Now the term overwhelmed makes sense.

Now around my heart there's a fence.

I'm tired of trying to find my husband, he was never sent.

All of the "I love you's" you never meant.

Every I love you too I fight in my head.

Every night that you slept in my bed.

Permanent tears stain my eyes red,

and now every word that we said,

has shattered and now our love too is dead.

I remember how much meeting your family meant.

Since I can't take you with me, you have to be left.

I try to suppress the day that we met.

I loved you until I had no love left.

With you now gone I love you no less.

It's just so hard to clear your mind when your heart is a mess.

Words-4-tha-Wise- How To Know It's Safe To Date Again:

1. When you are confident and secure with yourself as a single person

2. When you no longer feel obligated to remain faithful to your ex in hopes of reconciliation

3. When you are no longer angry with any partner from your past

4. When you almost never reminisce on relationships from the past

5. When you are happy about your life and decisions belonging to only you

6. When you are capable of having fun on your own or simply enjoying your own company

7. When you have recovered long enough to be considered emotionally available

8. When you are willing and able to start a new relationship with a fresh mind

9. When you are secure enough within yourself to be able to trust others again

10. When you no longer live in fear of what a future relationship might bring

Pre-tension

I decided to act as though I could not be hurt by this man.

My plan was to stand strong long enough and always hold on to his hand.

I intended for him to be my man and my man only.

I decided to act as though it didn't hurt on nights he would leave me lonely.

I needed the soul of a broken man to come around and console me.

Not control me.

A man not so man enough that he would always ask for permission.

A man not so man enough that he would love me with conditions.

A man who loved his momma so much he would invite me to family traditions.

I would try to condition the way he would love me.

Make sure I accepted nothing above me.

Knowing all along that he could never hug me with a straight face,

because my black man apparently doesn't prefer his own race.

My black man has a list of bitches he needs to chase.

My black man has no issue with lying to my face;

With staying in my place.

Yet always on his way somewhere else.

Always reserving time to spend with someone else.

Always leaving me to feel as though there was someone else.

When all I could ever think about was him and no one else.

No one helps when the deceit is all you can think about.

I force myself to suppress the fact that there's someone else that he tends to think about.

I run away from reality because there are better things to think about.

Other People's Problems

But then I return to this empty house and you're the only one I seem to think about.

I hated that when you told the truth you were lying,

and that you were so dramatic when denying,

that your heart would beat in more than one place,

and these lips that I kiss have touched her face.

The sex I would get you probably fucked her the same day;

in the same way.

Heart ache always hurts the best,

when your mind is desperate for some rest;

when you're just about to clean that mess;

when you agree to stay together and try to progress;

when your money seems to become less and less;

and when all your homegirls know your every stress.

What am I supposed to do now?

Oh yea do me.

As if I'm excited about him exiting my life right now.

As if I'm supposed to fuck my way to clarity somehow.

Or act like it's cool that you were never mine somehow.

How unfair it is.

I'm ready to go fuck up a ratchet bitch.

Beat her ass and who ever she dealin with.

Fuck you up for not knowing who you were messing with.

Then put it in a poem and act like I never did.

I'm sorry your daddy never loved you.

Sorry your two baby mommas couldn't hug you strong enough,

and I'm sorry my heart wasn't strong enough to carry you.

I really thought that one day I would marry you,

but now I have enough baggage to bury you.

Good bye my love;

I wish I never loved you either.

<u>Words-4-tha-Wise-How To Start Recovering From A Bad Breakup:</u>

1. Accept that you will have to go through pain in order to heal

2. Change your habits and surroundings

3. View your breakup as a challenge to do and pick better next time

4. Spend time around someone you admire

5. See this time alone as an opportunity for personal growth

6. Do not project hate onto their character

7. Remember the bad times when your try to reminisce on the good

8. Take this time to understand your own emotions so that you can better protect yourself

9. Keep on believing in love

10. Be happy and laugh everyday

Please Go Away

Please don't write me to say hello.

Nor should you just be saying goodnight.

I understand that you still miss us and that's ok because so do I.

But right now my thoughts they ache from you.

I'm sifting through every lie you put me through.

Still wondering what the fuck I could have done to you,

to make you believe that I would ever be ok with losing you;

In this way.

On the day before my dad's birthday.

Promptly after kissing my forehead and anticipating your presence like any other day.

Now I try to forget you.

Every hour is another head space to get through,

and every minute I think of the times I gave you the keys to what I thought opened every door inside of me.

I let you in believing you wouldn't have to hide from me.

I know your lie and now I can't sleep quietly.

I miss the ways that you would hold me.

I miss hearing your voice every time you told me that you loved me.

Wanted to be with me,

wanted a family with me,

but when did we include her?

How is it that she somehow came first?

How is it that she now makes my life worse simply by knowing who I am today?

Other People's Problems

Why the fuck does this bitch know where the fuck I stay?

I started to look for both of you that day.

I now see she was only trying to get in the way.

You see in the midst of her being a bitch,

she tracked me down to tell me about you.

Sent me pictures that, still to this day, make me sick.

Even went on to say that you were her broke nigga while you were my all.

She speaks of you as though you were nothing at all.

When I tried to be your comfort when the world made you feel small.

Now I do admit that I was never perfect.

I stayed out all night sometimes on purpose.

I even let a few others get passed the surface,

but I never gave them sex.

I would never come make love to you then love them next.

Now all of the weekends I left you in my house I regret.

I regret that I trusted you at all.

I hate that I said yes to this relationship and all.

I never knew a man could make you feel so small.

Or like all the love you gave meant nothing at all.

You lied about who she was to you.

You even reported back to her what I would say to you.

Lying about your plentiful deceitful nights like I would never find the truth.

I hate that I thought I could trust you.

Even more for the fact that I still love you.

I pray to miss you as though you never existed.

Other People's Problems

I pray you use protection to protect you from the viscous.

But in my life the only way I can seem to get through this,

is to just move on and act like like our love never existed.

I don't plan to date other men inspite you.

I'm not even writing this poem to fight you.

I understand that you're a man with feelings that slipped up on more than one night boo.

She was your night boo.

I was your sleep.

Every time you would leave me I could feel the deceit.

The sex drive seemed to stop because I knew you would cheat.

I just wanted to believe in our forever but now that can't be.

It seems as though we are not for each other.

It seems that next time I should listen to my mother.

It seems that this time you should read this and always know,

that even though I hate you I will always love you though.

Even though I hate you I will never let it show.

Apparently I suck at being vulnerable.

But now you can know.

Maybe after some time has passed I'll invite you to be my friend.

Not that I need you anymore,

but all of your random "I just want to say hi's" can find a garbage disposal to go jump in.

I wish I could invite you back just for the sex.

Sleep with you one night then ignore you the next.

Then act like it's ok to get back with my ex;

but that will end badly-- Sadly.

Words-4-tha-Wise- How To Create Boundaries For Ex's:

1. Understand that it is ok and mandatory to set boundaries

2. Acknowledge that things that are unacceptable to you should no longer be accepted

3. If necessary let the other person know that there are lines that they can no longer cross and enforce that

4. Expect to feel discomfort while cutting people off, or limiting your interaction

5. Remain consistent

6. Remember the pain and the reason why it was necessary to create boundaries in the first place

7. Temporary pleasure will only increase the depth of the pain

8. Make sure you respect your boundaries by not crossing over from your side as well

9. Do not let your boundaries turn into a form of control

10. Believe in your unique value as an individual; treat yourself as if you were brand new

Follow The Light

I just feel like I love alone,

Alongside the sadness that is magnified by the definition of being depressed.

I am sad and unbelievably.

I'm disappointed that I'm starting not to believe in me.

I'm remembering the part where I start harboring my presence.

Where I become no longer present.

No longer will I know how to exist.

In fact I fear I won't even be missed,

and the man that kissed me yesterday said he was leaving.

I'm starting to understand my love hurts because my mind is deceiving.

You see I was dreaming of the life I thought we would live,

and meanwhile reality,

without an aspirin to give says wake up Ashley!

That is not correct!

Love is NOT your project!

You must make a way somehow.

I must commit to something and like now,

and I have no time to fall behind on anything.

I have one year of school left and I just got done failing everything.

I took some time to became my own boss while still paying the cost of being a working woman.

Sacrificing time for creativity.

stalling the moments that slowly deliver me to a realm called everything I am.

Other People's Problems

I fear so often the woman I can be.

I worry so often about the problems I can't see,

but I can't see an ending to my indecision,

when my heart can be so heavily imprisoned,

by love and all of the selfish things.

Be willing to give up my drive and all of my precious things,

so that I can feel yet another warm hello,

but a punctual heartbreaking goodbye.

Another invitation to cry.

Another Hail Mary begging my heart not to die,

my mouth not to lie about how I may be ok.

Even when it means the world may feel a way.

I started with dreams of financial wealth,

and now I'm stumbling upon a spiritual self that is finding health in communication.

Finding reason for constant vibrations.

Finding reasons to make it to specific destinations so that I know my soul can receive love for a while.

Where that thing on my face is an intentional smile,

and where I haven't laughed in a while turns into everything is beautiful and every human is gifted.

May every spirit be lifted if it be low.

Never be ashamed and know that love can exist in the fog.

Trust and believe that God has something planned for you.

Be sad but find a place where you are welcome to,

sit and say you feel like shit,

while sharing with others your mental gifts of being a surviving example,

so that if there is someone else out there who might feel trampled.

Know that I know that I don't know if it will be ok.

But at least you are sitting here with me today,

and for once in awhile you'll probably get to voice how you really feel;

because these feelings they really feel.

<u>Words-4-tha-Wise- How To Be Optimistic During Hard Times:</u>

1. Understand that hard times come to test your stamina and endurance

2. Complete five things for each subject everyday: 1- Career, 2- Community, 3- Family, 4- Home improvement, 5- Your spirit

3. View your upcoming obstacles as challenges

4. Look for ways to cut down on financial spending

5. Exercise

6. Pursue your favorite hobby

7. Seek out cheap or free entertainment

8. Cook your own food

9. Give to others who are in need

10. Gain a tighter grasp on the things that are really important to you in your life

Emotional Avoidance

For those of you who are afraid to feel,

you are choosing to live with scabs that will never learn to heal.

You are opting for a lifestyle that is anything but real.

To feel is to explore the ocean floor of your mind.

To feel is to provide leverage for the wasters of your time.

When we walk amongst others with our pain left unfixed,

our problems left unrecognized,

and with curses upon our lips,

we begin to normalize danger and now the lesson you were suppose to learn is now missed.

You have now convinced your urges to try on just any show that may fit.

Your emotions are your reminder.

They are your biological timer,

alarming you to unwelcome persons,

and situations that may make your life worsen.

Your feelings visit you as your heart in person.

your emotions speak to your cheeks in the form of tear drops,

watering your pores until your heart is done breaking.

To be out of your feelings is like making the decision to ignore your check engine light.

You are making the conscious decision to leave light to further enjoy harmful hum of darkness,

and I don't believe that confusion is where your heart is;

and I don't believe that if you are troubled that you want this.

I urge you to believe in the magic that you experience,

you will build useful experience like touching a stove while it's hot.

Your heart will remind you of what not to do.

Your aching soul can do a lot for you.

To walk away from truth will place a block on you,

blocking you from better decisions haven't learned to make.

While neglecting your emotions you will blindly forsake your need to be free.

Your words will become counterfeit and you will cast spells on all you see.

You will be the example of what it is like to flee,

and when it's time to be strong your mental muscles will remain weak.

Your mindless actions will attach to your days.

You will deflect love and positive rays.

Then your mind will become sick of your ways.

Your mind will grow weary from your lies.

Forming disbelief in self before you even begin to try;

your love will die.

Give yourself constant reminders that your thoughts are you internal portal,

transferring your psyche to plains untouched by mortals.

they give you time and space to get your mind in order,

giving your permission to evacuate negativity and freeloaders.

And when you think those thoughts ask yourself why you think that way?

Acknowledge that your thoughts are a reflection of you and they will continue to be that way.

You should be taking more time to feel and pray.

The meditation from your heart will bring freedom to your days.

Other People's Problems

If your feelings begin to haunt you on your journey send positivity and love that way,

and by way I mean in that specific direction.

To experience the trauma from your pain will bring your protection.

To be out of your feelings is the equivalent to spiritual neglection.

To forget how to feel is to forget how to think.

Your confidence, self esteem, and sense of reality will sink.

Your feelings are what tie you to your life; they are your missing link.

feeling your feelings will push you over the brink of what you thought was impossible.

Your emotions are not a deterrent they make progress possible.

Your feelings will become capable of understanding the logical.

To ignore how you feel is to ignore is to ignore yourself.

Process the pain til all of your demons melt.

Feel bad til you feel better; feel til you find your better self.

Words-4-tha-Wise- How To Grow Strength From All Of Your Problems:

1. Understand that struggle builds character

2. Build a support team for your life/business

3. Always find positivity in any situation

4. Keep a journal and a planner

5. Experience nature

6. Make a list of all of things you would like to accomplish in this life

7. Use confident language

8. Plan out your days

9. Be still and know that everything will be ok

10. Rewrite the story of who you really are-- A WARRIOR!!!

Other People's Poems

Mitch Shaw:

The Male Review

I knew who you were, and it terrified me

Anxious, excited, nervous over what we could be

I knew you were different when you ignored my shenanigans

I knew you were special when I couldn't wait to see you over and over again

I didn't know I wasn't ready

I didn't know I wasn't steady

I was hiding from ghosts and demons

Blaming your love for all the wrong reasons

Closed off and guarded

Coming off cold hearted

You didn't deserve the trouble and pain

For all the confusion going on in my brain

Other People's Problems

I didn't deserve your time or your love

Now I'm fighting to keep myself above

Without you it feels like I'm drowning

Watching the minutes go, counting

The days till you leave my life forever

Along with my smile for never

Will i forgive myself if I love you

I know now what is true

I don't have to be scared

I can be vulnerable and bare

Story of a Man Who Was Closed Off and Woke Up To His Mistakes

Words never said

Lie in feelings that are dead

1,440 minutes a day, 7 days a week

I commit to quiet and living meek

I'm tired

I'm done

I have no desire to run

And chase wild thoughts of passion

Or inquire about today's love fashion

No more paying the inflated costs

Going broke over emotional loss

I'm tired

I'm done

Promise

Honest

Don't look at me with sad eyes and thoughts or prayers

This is not a declaration stemmed from dissonance or despairs

The wings are clipped and Cupid has lost his aim

Allowing for clarity and focus to remain

I'm tired

I'm done

Honest

Promise

Indifferent

Quiet

Myesha Mitchell

Beyoncé You Ain't Shit

I'm Sitting here listening to this song I ain't sorry by Beyoncé and never thought that it would ever apply to me,

but I found out that I'm actually dealing with a real life situation of a Becky.

You know Becky with the good hair, Becky with the pretty colored eyes, Becky with the skinny body.

Becky taking what I thought was mine and only belonged to me, ok wait, well not exactly.

I'll admit to you, that she kinda had him first, but see he explained that she was just an obsessed ex.

But after a year of us dating, let me explain the foolishness that happened next.

I welcomed him into my home, and even treated his children as if they were mine.

I understood that she was his recent pass and assumed that her existence would fade away in due time.

Other People's Problems

There were the nights that he didn't come home, and the times he even avoided my calls.

But it never occurred to me that someone he claimed he hated would be the reason our relationship would fall.

Subliminal messages she'd put on social media, the certain things she'd say and know.

He claimed that communication with them was very limited, but she knew way too much about me tho.

She knew where I lived exactly, where I worked and even who I associated with.

So who else is at fault for her being this so informed FBI detective bitch??

My personal situations she spoke on as if she literally heard it from my own mouth.

I was puzzled to how she knew about things that was secretly occurring within my house.

Late night and early morning calls to his phone.

He always excused it by saying it was about his children, so I often left the situation alone.

Than it would hit me and I would question why, because she wasn't even the mother to any of his MANY kids.

But then at the same time I would support it because she stepped up and was doing things that even the children's own mothers never did.

But it also put me in the state of insecurity, because how did he expect me to step up if he never made her step down.

How was I supposed to be their mother figure, if he still felt it was appropriate for her to be around.

He'd make his comments often about my children's father, saying he needed to be less in the picture, insinuating as if he was trying to step up and play dad.

But the difference that he never grabbed the concept of, was that kids together, him and Becky never ever had.

Other People's Problems

Congratulations Becky, you've done good. Now back the hell off and let us be,

but the thing he never told me, was that it was he who couldn't set her free.

Found out later that when we'd get into our little fights and disagreements, to her is where he went.

She couldn't have been making this shit up, because she even screen shot me all the messages that he sent.

It's hurtful because the dates and times says that he sent those messages while he was laying up next to me.

Fucking me good, while expressing how much he loved me, but sending her I miss you texts after he put my ass to sleep.

Family vacations, and spending plenty of time together, yea we did all of that. Posting pictures on the internet for the world to see that it's us now and forever.

To only have her messy ass comment under the pictures saying shit like "you guys look good together."

He begged me not to entertain it, not to be bothered and not to feed into it.

But then she'd message me some receipts, proving that when he ignored me it's because it was her that he was with.

Her being funny asking me shit like how does her pussy taste, claiming that because the night before he had his face all in it.

Her Telling me that she's not the problem, and that it's he who keeps making her relevant.

He began to use her being the only mother figure his children knew as an excuse.

But if I'm who he's claiming to want to marry, what would be my role, what did he expect for me to do.

See he'd make it a point to tell me that exs were a thing of the past.

And that if their presence was important than those relationships would have lasted.

He'd tell me that from my previous relationship that I hadn't fully moved on.

And would tell me that he and I would never be completely happy until all my feelings for my ex were completely gone.

But see I'd sit in front of him with no hesitation and compose a text to my exs, telling them that I was happy with who I was currently with.

But couldn't get this nigga to do the same. I couldn't even get him to block the bitch.

In his phone, her number was still saved.

There was even still a picture stored in the contact picture place.

My mom said I was being naive, that I was just accepting his bullshit because I wanted to feel like I was complete.

He never brought a damn thing to the table,

he would never be the full package, his loyalty would never fully be with me.

Because she did for him what I would never, she accepted and made excuses for who he was.

She even encouraged his way of living, and she even supported him in his decision to indulge in drugs.

but of course she would and of course she did, because together they are both drug addicts.

Then she tried to throw in my face that I was bipolar and an alcoholic.

Did that bother me, no not really. Because after years of being in denial, I accepted me for me and I was far from being embarrassed.

I used to hate who I was, and I used alcohol to mask my feelings.

But is that junkie on life support really trying to call out the way someone else is living??

Becky you can have him, together you two crack heads can live happily ever after.

Stop watching my damn Facebook, you won, I seriously don't want him. But I'm sure to your insecure ass that doesn't matter.

and yea BITCH I seen your car parked outside my house the other night, wrong place, wrong girl, he's not with me.

Other People's Problems

I'm assuming he didn't come home last night, and didn't answer his phone, so that's why you're out here on the creep.

Trust I'm out the picture completely,

I was done before I even informed you.

See the difference between you and I, I was seriously done when I told you both that I was through.

I promise I'm not an issue, please don't allow me to be one of your insecurities or one of your worries.

This Nubian Queen has tilted her crown to you, and I've accepted the fact that we've lost another black man to another fucking Becky.

<u>Patiently Waiting</u>

You told me to be patient, and let everything happen naturally,

Only you left me standing in one spot,

And never came back for me.

You promised that everything would be ok, and that eventually together we'd be great.

Than you did things that weren't acceptable,

And put the blame on me by telling me that my timing was too late.

You indecisively tagged me along,

While exploring your many options.

And took it upon yourself to not tell me to enter the situation with severe precaution.

Because you didn't know what you wanted,

It was I who took a loss.

You only protected yourself,

And manipulated me into paying the cost.

In me you saw something worth taking, but I guess nothing worth to keep.

But you continued to string me along, and never cared that things would get this deep.

Now I'm in head over heels, and not a clue on what to do.

I can't believe you were that damn selfish, and only did what was best for you.

Other People's Problems

I told you about my past, and the things that I've been through.

You promised you were different and that your intentions were pure and true.

So where are you now, now that I'm still where you left me waiting.

Where's all the stuff you said would come along if I stood in one spot patiently.

How could I be so naive to think that you really had intentions of making me your girl.

To even think that someone like you was capable of giving me the world.

They say sometimes it's not what you know but that instead it's who,

And nothing about this was beneficial, so I wasted time in getting to know you.

Now I see, that more than likely I was just one of the many.

And between us all, promises you probably told plenty.

I'm sure you'll get what all you deserve, whether it's good but hopefully bad.

You'll regret and see that Something real and consistent, with me is what you could of had.

You rolled the dice, took a chance, and your selfish ass felt that either way for you it was a win.

Although the grass may look greener on the other side, don't be surprised if the soil deceives and sucks you in.

Not that I'm intentionally lurking, but I often see you and the life that you have chose.

Are you really happy is what I question, but I guess we'll never know.

I'm not mad that you didn't choose me, just confused about why you made me wait.

You knew where you wanted to be all along, but made it seem like it was I who had too much on my plate.

Just fix this, then correct that, get your mind right and do what's best for you.

That's the type of shit you often told me, when in reality you already had your mind made on what you wanted to do.

I don't understand why you try to play check in, when I know you're only trying to see if how you left me is how I remained.

Like it's ok that you've moved on in life,

But that things between us are supposed to stay the same.

I have feelings too, just like her, but it's obvious that mines never mattered.

I guess you choosing her, but not fully letting me Go, I should be thankful better yet flattered.

She won I guess, she's got you, but still I'm standing where you left me.

Where's all the stuff you said would come along if stood in one spot patiently waiting???

DJ Lace

Borrowed

Borrowed man

On borrowed time

I know damn well

That you're not mine

But while you're here

Lie to me

Tell me I'm all yours

And you're all mine

With fire in your eyes

The girth between your thighs

And the moist between mine

lust overthrown our hearts

Other People's Problems

As we lie on this bed of roses

Forgetting the thorns

Ignoring what's really on our minds

Addicted to the feeling

Hoping these actions have meaning

Dreaming one day this may be realistic

But I'm too altruistic

And you're just plain old selfish

Knowing this is only for a short time

And the physical

May be sensual

For that moment in time

But once my heart is open

I realize you're only joking

Playing the game

And winning the prize

Cuz when I look in your eyes

I never see forever

Only this moment in time

And once it's over

I lay waiting

But it never comes

You finish and

You roll to your side

And I swallow my pride

Other People's Problems

As I redress

Feeling foolish for thinking this sex was for me

Now full of stupidity

I sense the cold cruel reality of my existence

As only one of many pawns

I will never be your only

But I still wish to one day become

The Queen of your heart

Other People's Problems

DJ Almond Eyez

Live From El Cajon

I'm reportin the news

It's about 100 degrees

Pavement burning my shoes

We just arrived on the scene

They blocked off the section

The cops looked ready for war

Heavily armed with weapons

We hesitated

Crowd looked like they had been baited

surrounded, Barricaded

on all sides

Like a box by the cops

So we thought

Let's go shut down the mall

If dead black bodies don't matter

Other People's Problems

It will when yo pockets fall

So we busted a U quick

Turned on some music

Started chanting

Yelling "fuck 12"

While we movin

All united

No intentions to start a riot

But fuck all of that being quiet

It's a war outside shit

Better pick a side before it's chosen for you

We marched down the street against the system

Cuz we know that's the truth

I held hands with my sister

Like the two ladies before us

Screamin no justice no peace

Just like the ones before us

This is war

This is war

We get farther down the street

See the eyes in the sky

While we're burning in the heat

We get farther down the street

We are where the freeway meets

And then that's when we see we're met with a line of police

Other People's Problems

They had batons and guns

tazers, helmets, and shields

They even brought out some dogs

That they told to heel

So we paused and regrouped

Then Linked arms and walked

The onlookers stood by

While hella camera crews stalked

We got closer to the babylons

Thinkin why you blockin all the roads that I pay taxes on

Then they clinched their batons

And started yellin some shit

We kept on marchin forward

We knew It was bout to get lit

The cops looked like the military

The only ones thats lookin scary

All the time I'm thinkin

Fuck I'm about to open carry

What a coward

This aint power

What are you without the badge

Alfred Olango was a black man

Black Just like my dad

We live less than 10 miles away

How do I know we are safe

Other People's Problems

Feel like I'm going insane

This shit can weigh on your brain

We were on the other side

They wouldn't let us pass by

They protected the businesses

More than they protected our lives

They say revolution isnt televised

But it was on facebook live

Sakea Martin

Black Girl Wakes Up

Black girl Rises

Shakes off her comforter of armor & steps on to the battlefield.

She draws back the blinds questioning if she's ready for another day.

Rays sear through the window pane.

Black girl debates if the heat is meant to warmly caress her awakened melanin or torch her loud existence to quiet ash.

Black girl remembers how she used to be afraid of the dark, seek solace in the sun, but now white light shoots in like the enemy.

Other People's Problems

Black girl, procrastinates her daily routine of surgery, drags resisting flesh to the mirror.

Black girl confronts her reflection and is reminded she is still black.

She slides a steady hand over coiled curls & plump lips

Notices how over the years

The way her stomach sits

Thick Hips curve

& booty pokes

Make her look more woman

Yet her face make her look more bullseye

Post-dissection

Black girl goes to bathroom to wash herself off /

She cleanses her face of unrealistic beauty standards /

Rinses her mouth of self hatred /

Looks up and catches the fleeting glimpse of a survivor

Black girl goes to get dressed. Drapes her body in plain clothing, laces up dirty sneakers.

Black girl cradles a navy blue baseball cap in one hand and a kente head wrap in the other.

She imagines she can hide all 5 ft nothing of her behind the brim of the cap

Other People's Problems

Be inconspicuous.

Less suspicious.

Then maybe America won't stare in her direction

But they'll probably notice her cowering

Assume it's for a reason

Mistake her hat for weapon, a criminals disguise

Black girls shield could become ammunition's excuse

Maybe she should just rock the wrap

Adorn her crown with patterns

Secure tradition with knots

Hold her head a little higher

But then,

Will her royalty offend them?

Will her being unapologetically black offend them?

She fears they will misinterpret her black girl magic

Confuse it for some type of show

Note her confident defiance

After they kill her for entertainment

Black girl wonders should she evade being seen or carry herself as queen?

Either way, won't her existence provoke them?

Ronald Williams

Hands

These hands are lovers

Two ribboned balloons

Waiting to fly into your existence

These hands are

Bed spread comforters

To Lay

Your body under

Palms show the journey I've traveled

Just to find you

Knuckles,

Staggered with Blood

From times

When I beat myself

Other People's Problems

Into submission

This black complexion

Archiving

Novels

That my ancestors

Were not granted

Permission to read

When you ask to hold my hands

I grip your fingers

Like beach sand

Sinking into Sunset

Between

Your ears

Caress

The crescent moons

You resume

To call fingernails

Grip parts of you

The way eve's hands suctioned forbidden fruit

If touching you was a sin

I'd pray to the wind

That levitated your touch

And inform God

Of my new savior

My hands wish

Other People's Problems

To hold your existence

The way gravity holds

Planets

The way gravel holds black bodies

But this is not about

Police brutality

You are no prisoner

To these hands

That dance

To the rhythm

Of your curiosity

My skin melts

Everytime you touch me

Our bodies collide

And for the first time

I felt pangea

Through the pores

Of our hands

Your fingers cripple

My body into canvas

Each picture worth 1000 words

Let's dip these fingers

Into common interest

And paint our future

With these hands.

Kovu

They Say Niggas Ain't Shit

but,

Ain't that what they wanted you to believe?

Was that not the plan when they removed our fathers and replaced them with the stereos and stereotyped TV?

Teaching us young that the only men left were in the streets.

So if we missed daddy and yearned for a role model that is most likely where he would be.

Do you not see?

Show and tell only to have truths quilled and stuffed in box taped shut and labeled excuse then wonder why we don't open up.

Fuck excuses the simple truth is, we aren't allowed to acknowledge the symptoms of our abuses or the effects of neglect nor emotional misuses.

If a tree falls down in the forest does it make a sound? Yes. But not true sound you; see Einsiten's theory of relativity states sound is a two part phenomenon vibrations go out and must be receipted.

If a man cries out abandonment issues and you make him daddy without first healing was his warning not sounded.

Other People's Problems

My masculinity has learned fragility from a society created to encourage the ruthless while ignoring where the ruthless are rooted.

Cause you see it's a well known fact that niggas ain't shit period. That's it.

I heard a poet say "brainwashing isn't hard it's just takes a little repetition."

So before you continue to make blanket statements that we are all comparable to feces, question whose lyrics you spit.

Ghost written cantations spoken to manifest our damnation.

Studies show if you speak negativity into plant it stunts its growth and eventually literally dies from the words you speak.

And they don't speak our language so what do you think will happen to me?

Joan 'Lyric' Leslie

More Black Girl than Magic

The older white woman on the M.A.R.T.A. looks at me with questions in her eyes Like she's does not quite know how to form them or if I'm the right one to pose them to

She sits with a shy tongue,

which I perceive to be a first

Looks wise enough to interpret my face to be a combination of: Not today Satan & This ain't what ya want

She proceeds to look at me like she just can't understand how this fro goes to work with a fly ass business suit and heels

A nose ring on Friday's & a coffee mug just because

Like she really wanna ask: Ha-ha-ha-How your hair do that thing where it transforms over night?

And you go from Jill Scott to a Michelle Obama look alike?

How your braids touch down to your waistline in the summertime?

How your edges so slick but the rest of your hair so disobedient?

Defying gravity?

Laughing in the face of blow dryers and most other forms of heat?

Other People's Problems

How does it assimilate and acclimate to its conditions as fast as you do?

Like how y'all go from Harlem to the Ivy League?

How is your English as good as it is but it still blends in with both the hoods of North America and the still winds of New Hampshire?

HOW YOU DO IT, GIRL?

How you turn lemons into lemonade?

Oodles-of-Noodles into Olive Garden with cheese and whatever's in that cabinet?

Toast that wonder bread slice before you realize everything white is bad for you:

White bread

white rice

white sugar

white people

Or before you realize that's really just your mother's way of saying: diabetes is killing this family faster than white people

How Momma sooo health conscious but still got hypertension?

How Momma make it to 60?

How she make it to 30 without no babies in the projects?

How you make it 27 with no babies in the hood?

How you make it out the hood but your accent camouflage itself into varying forms of blackness?

How you do it girl?

How you wake up with a smile on as big as the sun when you were just up crying the night before?

How this woman on the M.A.R.T.A. look at you every morning and don't know what you really look like sad?

How you hide pain in your Lyrics?

Other People's Problems

Lyrics in your name?

And they still don't know that pain is yours?

How you mask heartbreak girl?

How you fascinate yourself with the Gucci Mane-like glow up afterwards?

How you recover like Obama after 8 years of conservative stress in his mane?

How you deal with the guilt of voting for Jill to replace him Knowing you ain't never really trust them white girls?

How you bounce back from your political setback with a poem about how you ain't never really trust them white girls?

And have them white girls writin' they own poems about how they can't be trusted?

How ya pen made outta blood, sweat, tears & magic?

How ya pen turn this heavy load this weight of the world into magic?

How You do it girl?

How You do it girl?

How You do it girl?

I'd tell you if I thought you could handle it

wouldn't try to colonize it and call it home

But 10 times out of 9 I know you'd be lying

Know you wouldn't know what to do with all this gift

This shea butter stack of secrets

So to the older white woman on the Marta who stares perplexed at all of this complexity Who I just assume wants to know ('Cause don't they all really just want to know?)

But the answer to the question you've been pondering Is disrespectfully rhetorical in its purest form: It asks & answers itself all in the same breath:

233

How am I more Black Girl than magic, but have still managed to convinced the world otherwise

Other People's Problems

Carrie E.

Shout Out To Pain

Pain, it hurts me to even speak of you

I'm not really sure how we met or which headache gave you my address

But I'm tired

I thought my wounds would heal properly

I believed that you needed to be here

so I saved you a seat

I believe the first time I met you,

I was three years of age and couldn't recognize you,

I couldn't recognize that you needed me to be strong in order to subside
the feeling you bring

Now 18 years later I see you still remember me

Well remember me

I'm done submitting myself to you

Yes I know you will know me forever,

Other People's Problems

but now while you attack my nervous system,

my faith will medicate every wound you scar me with

But before you go

Leave the scars

Leave the love that I believe was mine

Leave the "you will never amount to anything's"

Leave the family and friends that wronged me

Leave the memories of my soul

Leave the tears

Leave the false hope

Leave the lies

Leave the heartache

Leave the fear

Most importantly,

leave me you

So when I finally fall in love with me,

I'll match my soul to you.

Other People's Problems

Monisha McNeely

Bare

I'm not good enough

I give love but you want to give up

Im replaceable

To love me back incapable

You regret me

I beg you to stay with me

You wish you didn't have children with me

The greatest gifts you've given to me

You won't be the man you said you would be

Promises you easily broke with me

You won't marry me

Hurts to know you don't see a future with me

I'm not a good woman to you

Or so you say

Other People's Problems

But I base my life around you each and everyday

I'm not taking care of my responsibilities as a mother

Or so you say

But I'm exhausted from taking care of them each and everyday

I make you do these things to me

I push you to wanna cheat

I'm a bitch

My opinion don't mean shit

You want to hit me

But something is stopping you

I never helped you

Even though I gave you my life

I based our relationship off being your wife

I didn't need a ring to commit because your love was all I ever needed

Now you're gone once again

I lost my love and my best friend

I really thought we would make it

My heart felt like it was just starting to mend

But you ripped it out my chest and crushed it with your bare hands.

Other People's Problems

Amber Johnson

Lone Road

No father Lost Mother

May I please roll for another

Dark streets with no path just me acting her ass

everything taught matched nothing that's shown

still a little girl with Integrity and a heart of Stone

Settlement tickets given for the abandonment

within came by the stack

yes this is a fact

I'll give my everything and more right off of my back

begging for love off of anyone's track

Other People's Problems

expose me to my community who have my back

still yet I lack and search to fill the void

only to try and try and fail

Yes I'm annoyed

angry and Confused

but I can't stay down even though me staying down was just a thought

it was a thought that was 2 seconds too long

words ringing you're strong you're smart

you got this, yeah that part

Continuously I just want to be a part of the trees that make me AMB

E for excellent

R cuz please put some respect on it

accepting the love security and loyalty that comes so artificially

allows me to bear real fruit leaving no need to ever diss you

just know

forever and always I still will miss you

Other People's Problems

Stephanie Reyes

From a very young age, we girls are taught, shown, grown, told, that we must learn our place and fit into this societal female mold, how to be:

-Be bold, but not too bold; don't want to offend anyone

-Be kind, even when you are being taken advantage of, or treated poorly

-Be smart, unless your intelligence challenges that of an entitled man

-Be fit, but not too fit, muscles make you look masculine; vanity, not health, is the goal

-Be beautiful, but just the right amount, not slutty or overly confident; that shit's a turn off

-Be generous, but only if others are watching, it's convenient, or if we can post it on the internet

-Be empowering, but only on the outside, it's ok to secretly hate, tear down, or covet another woman's accomplishment

This is how I'm supposed to be?

This makes me angry, confused, hurt, and ambivalent. Secretly, if I'm honest, part of me wants this and loathes myself for it. What is this human condition to be at odds with oneself?

-What if they knew this information?

241

Other People's Problems

-What if I am not good enough?

-What if I fail as a mother?

-What if he leaves me?

-What if I never achieve my goals, my dreams?

-What if that societal mold is who I am?

-What if this is all there really is?

What if, what if, what if, what if?

Till my mind is consumed by them, taking up every ounce of space.

Till I glow with self-doubt, insecurity, and shame.

Enough!

Be still, quiet this anxious heart.

Breathe!

The world has enough negativity, criticism, and hate. Let it not begin in me.

Breathe, breathe, breathe; be still.

Why focus on the negative? Why doubt yourself? Why fall for the comparison trap?

-Breathe, this is how I'm supposed to be

-Be kind, have compassion

-Be bold, stand for something

-Be strong, enough to live

-Be smart, lend your knowledge to come up with solutions to the issues

-Be fit, to enjoy life and live in health

-Be generous, just because

-be beautiful, let your soul be what others see

-Be empowering, we need more love

-Be present, put down your phone and enjoy this moment

Other People's Problems

Just be you!

For I am I, and I am me.

This thing called life, you only get one shot. Let's finish strong by helping one another, because in the end the things won't matter; the memories, the relationships, they are what holds true.

I'll be me.

You'll be you.

Savor these fleeting moments.

Be the hope you need in this world.

God bless!

Frailty

That bitch visits me

And takes a strangle hold of my fears and turns my fears into nightmares.

Nightmares those ridiculous pile of hormones that leave me shattered and distraught, like real life isn't cruel enough,

My psyche must create even more death and destruction to torment me.

I refuse to give fear and pain any more power over me.

If only my traitorous heart would believe it wasn't real.

Other People's Problems

Cheryl Key

FB/IG: @AuthorAshleyNicole
AuthorAshleyNicole12@gmail.com

right here

real

me stand tall as towers,

calm as the enchanted Living Water.

You are

ty as raging oceans and seas.

e given back my smile,

once   placed has returned full, bright, wide.

Remembered and reminded of what God's Love looks and feels like.

"I see Him in you."

Large blotches of darkness etched in my heart and soul like black holes

But You saw right through

Other People's Problems

With just one thought of You

And Your amazing Love

My spirit is now revived with it

plus, faith, trust, truth, grace, mercy, feeling, hope, healing.

oh,

how I could go on and on.

This is what I miss. This is what I've missed.

That feeling of, whenever I leave Your presence, I never should have left it!

For You were with me always.

Your radiance I felt upon me

left like breadcrumbs to a child lost, I've found my home in and with You, again.

I let You in.

Your welcoming arms speaking above all sound and voices,

They wrap around me as swaddling clothing,

comfort and safety is what is given in them when you hold me.

I am humbled to bask in Your glow.

Release what was and is no more.

Many will not comprehend the love I have for You.

Many will mock and laugh ridiculously, believe no such Love exists.

some will grasp that Love tightly and some will just let it slip away,

I am one of the Few that will hold on and never let go.

Each time I feel myself slip

I'll hear You,

say "For I know the thoughts I think toward you."

Miguel El Gran Tomás

You Motherfuckas Aint Shit

Claiming to be conscious but you ain't got no conscience.

We are so edified to the point that we ain't got no common sense

Running around whooping and hollering talking about this that and another but our environment is indicative on the fact that you truly don't give a damn about your brother

Yes a type of black man is valued and revered maybe if you have the height good hair green eyes and got a nice cup size and you strapped cash wise you gone get between them thighs and she will even let shit slide as black men we are completely objectified

Y.M.F.A.S.

Why is it that beta males set the standard and anything that a real nigga says gets slandered?

These Motherfuckas ain't got no backbone every fiber of their being is pandering.

Y.M.F.A.S.

This Apolitical-ness seems to be OUR source of stress

We out here playing checkers and the these crackers out here playing chess

Other People's Problems

Tell me why we have allowed all other minority groups to have a bid in on our suffering meanwhile they are out here working for the collective as a cohesive unit self-governing while we are descendants of slaves individuals without agency out here every day still hustling

Y.M.F.A.S.

It is of no concern to me if you are African or Caribbean or Spanish black

You are not grounded in the American black experience so do me a favor and please quit masquerading around and misrepresenting us like that. There's a line of succession you can gone head and get in the back

Y.M.F.A.S.

We are stepping stones of this society

By History and heritage we are not the same if you are not getting a return financially or socially then black folks we should stop laying claim

As Miss Maxine Waters at this moment we must reclaim our time and move forward by building healthy relationships amongst each other and we should be just fine

As black people we have a collective responsibility to do right by each other and if this is not put into practice generations will continue to suffer

Y.M.F.A.S.

Poverty is genocide you have two choices have children in poverty and be deemed irresponsible or don't reproduce and live comfortable

So I don't let anyone get close enough to me to disappoint me

this leaves me with no other choice but to drill THOTS until I find my queen

So I guess I ain't shit either.

A Man's Anxiety

You've captured my heart from the start

I know that I'm wrong but with you I feel right

I'm lost without you,

you are my eyes you are my light my love my life

my future wife

the mere thought of you is perfection perfecting

banter yes but you Bring it out of me

the willing of the power you possess is likened to a malady

I don't possess the acumen I'm only a man

the only way to be whole is by placing my life in your hands

But what makes something that seems so easy

be so hard

Why is it like T.YC. (Taking Your Charge)

taking a charge for a person

with uncertainty of the capacity to love just as hard

Kenslow Smith

The Present

There once was a competition between past, present, and future. The three challenged one another to determine who was the greatest to the humans.

Past said, "I am the greatest because I can be a constant supply of good feelings and emotions; I provide nostalgia."

Future said, "I am the greatest to humans because I provide motivation for aspirations and goals, I can be whatever they want me to be no matter how realistic, or unrealistic--I give them purpose."

Lastly, Present spoke. "Past, if you are not careful, then people lose their present and their future living in you." Present continued, "Future, if people are not careful their lives are consumed with you, constantly living in you they never really live at all."

Then Present said, "I am the greatest to humans because it is in me humans are most alive, for the past is frozen and the future has not yet come. It is I, the present, where humans experience all things from joy, to sorrow, in its purest form."

About the Author

Author Ashley Nicole (born Ashley Nicole Wilkins; April 12, 1989) is a Black American Author, Poet, Public Speaker, Actress, USMC veteran, active San Diego community member, and one third of Black Girl Magic Mini Market. She is best known for her scintillating poetry book, "The Death of a Serial Monogamist," that was originally published in September of 2015. Dubbed the "Queen of transparency", she has overwhelmed the spoken word culture with her life actualizing poetry, and has created a platform for other authors (creators) by starting her first publishing company (Sharing is Karen Publishing & Life Coaching), while presenting to you her second self-published work of truth, "Other People's Problems," and on her way to becoming a household name as she tours across the country. Several assessments regard her as one of the bold, innovative, and influential woman of her generation.

You may also contact Author Ashley Nicole via the following:

AuthorAshleyNicole12@gmail.com

SharingisKarenPublishingandLC@gmail.com

Other People's Problems

Instagram- @AuthorAshleyNicole

Facebook- Ashley Nicole Wilkins

45014406R10141

Made in the USA
Middletown, DE
13 May 2019